FIERCE & Unstoppable

My No BS True Story Of MS, Grief & Determination

CHARLIE HOVENDEN

Fierce & Unstoppable: My No BS True Story Of MS, Grief & Determination
© Charlie Hovenden 2025

www.charlieh.com.au

The moral rights of Charlie Hovenden be identified as the author of this work have been asserted in accordance with the Copyright Act 1968.

First published in Australia 2025 by Hovenden Enterprises Pty Ltd

ISBN 978-1-7643541-0-3

Any opinions expressed in this work are exclusively those of the author and are not necessarily the views held or endorsed by the Publisher.

All rights reserved. No part of this publication may be reproduced or transmitted by any means, electronic, photocopying or otherwise, without prior written permission of the author.

Disclaimer

All the information, techniques, skills and concepts contained within this publication are of the nature of general comment only and are not in any way recommended as individual advice. The intent is to offer a variety of information to provide a wider range of choices now and in the future, recognising that we all have widely diverse circumstances and viewpoints. Should any reader choose to make use of the information herein, this is their decision, and the author and publisher/s do not assume any responsibilities whatsoever under any conditions or circumstances. The author does not take responsibility for the business, financial, personal or other success, results or fulfilment upon the readers' decision to use this information. It is recommended that the reader obtain their own independent advice.

Dedicated to my loving husband, Brian, and my children, Josh & Hayley Hovenden.

"There is no greater agony than bearing an untold story inside you."

Maya Angelou

Preface

Close friends inspired me to write this book as they believed I had a story to tell. They felt people needed to hear about the journey I have endured to get here today.

We all get dealt a hand of cards, and it just depends whether or not you choose to win or lose. I have chosen to win, and winner takes all. Through strength, sadness, endurance, and positive thinking, I want to inspire others to believe that anything is possible if you put your mind to it.

I wrote this book because putting pen to paper helps to get your feelings out and becomes a very therapeutic exercise for the mind body and soul. I hope the journey of writing this book will be to inspire others that nothing is impossible in your life. I wish for you to experience all the personal challenges for myself and my family that we have endured to become the people we are today.

Friends and family have been the ones that have saved us through this – what seems an unjustifiable experience that we were given so unfairly to endure.

I especially want you, the reader, to realise how special it is to meet the one true love of your life. Unfortunately, this is not possible for everyone, but when if or it does happen, embrace it with every ember of your body because we just don't know how long we have it for.

Charlie x

Table of Contents

Preface vii

Introduction 1

Part 1: Growing Up As A Country Girl 7

    Chapter 1: My Small-Town Country Upbringing 9

    Chapter 2: Getting Into Trouble As A Teenager 19

    Chapter 3: My Sweet 16 39

    Chapter 4: Losing My Virginity 43

    Chapter 5: My Lifelong Best Friends 47

    Chapter 6: My Busy Family Life 57

    Chapter 7: Beginning My Work Life 67

    Chapter 8: Love At First Sight 79

    Chapter 9: Becoming Business Owners 95

Part 2: Living With MS 109

    Chapter 10: My Diagnosis 113

    Chapter 11: Medication 121

    Chapter 12: Learning to Live with My Disability 131

    Chapter 13: Constant Falls 139

    Chapter 14: Another Hospital Visit 145

Chapter 15: A Wedding In 45° Degree Heat 149

Chapter 16: Living with MS 153

Part 3: Brian Passing 159

Chapter 17: The Day It Happened 161

Chapter 18: The Funeral 177

Chapter 19: Getting Sick 189

Chapter 20: Grief & Loneliness 197

Chapter 21: Friends' Connection Post-Passing 203

Chapter 22: Remembering Him 211

Chapter 23: My Dark Thoughts 221

Chapter 24: Moving Forward vs Moving On 225

Conclusion 243

Acknowledgements 245

Introduction

I have written this book about my life story, telling you how my life began, as a young girl to a teenager, to a young adult, and now to an adult, growing up in a small town where you are related to everyone and the whole community knows your business. It is raw and real and honest – just like me. You will learn about the bad language, trust, determination, resilience, self-pity, grief, and strength that is needed to be able to come out the other side.

I am sharing my story because I want people to understand what I've been through. It's something that I just need to get out for myself. I hope to make people laugh and cry and just simply understand my journey. I hope to inspire people, to make them realise that anything is possible if you put your mind to it.

I went from being fit and athletic to not being able to walk without looking like I was drunk all the time (though, sometimes I probably was). I became relentlessly tired, and my coordination went completely up shit creek. I couldn't even throw a ball and catch it. What the fuck was happening to my body? I had no control over what was happening to me, which sent me into a head spin as I do NOT like losing control!

I landed the dream job, met the love of my life, and made lifelong friends. I had my little hobby farm and my children, but then the lightning and thunder crashed. When I was diagnosed with MS, a disabling disease, everything finally started to make sense, but I refused to let it beat me, so I stayed strong and positive. It gradually became worse, and I had treatment after treatment, but nothing helped. I very rarely spoke or whinged about my disease. I wasn't going to give it the pleasure of beating me. So, fuck you MS – you won't break my spirit!

But then the real kicker came. Life was great. Brian and I had our two children and were running a successful business, but we had obviously pissed someone off upstairs. Because one day, our lives changed forever. Brian died of an aneurysm. He collapsed at work in front of me. Then the kids had to watch the nightmare unfold before their, eyes which was like nothing you can ever imagine. Watching our hopes and dreams go up in smoke. I became a widow at 44 and the kids fatherless three weeks before their 18th and 21st birthdays. We all had to become different people to survive, but with great friends and family, we did it. Power of the mind is your strongest tool to have. It is what will be your saviour.

You will read about real life struggles with no fake-ass crap to hide behind. It is raw, with bare all on show for everyone to see and feel.

Unfortunately, life doesn't always smell like roses. Instead, it is drowned in the stench of bullshit, literally like it just dropped in your lap: a great big pile of crap just sitting there that dries up and falls apart while the blowies are buzzing around and just won't piss off. Believe me, I have been handed the fucking raw end of the deal and a huge shovel full of shit to go with it. Just one thing after another, and I kept wondering when I was finally going to get a break. It did cross my mind if it would ever stop. So I decided to snap out of it, use every part of my inner strength, and realise it was just another hurdle I had to jump over and get on with it. Toughen the fuck up, princess!

I've been to hell and back, and don't get me wrong: I still have plenty of bad and sad days, but thanks to Darren B and Bradley B, I have them to lean on constantly. But I am living proof that with positive thinking, determination, and resilience the devil can be kicked to the curb and told to fuck right off. My time is not over yet. I still have a life

Introduction

to live, and I plan to live it! So come along for the ride, it will be a fun and exhilarating one. I promise to show you a good time.

Just watch this space xx

A Little Bit About Charlie

Firstly, as the reader, you need to know a little bit about me to understand the book properly.

I am a country girl at heart. I grew up in a small country town on a farm with my family.

When I was 29, I was diagnosed with multiple sclerosis (MS). When I was older, I ran my own business, got married, and raised my two children. The big kicker, grief, entered when I lost my husband and my whole world.

To be clear, I don't want pity. I just want understanding. I just want people to know the truth, of how everything has unfolded, and what I have endured throughout my life. For the most part, I am a very strong person. But sadly, I can say I have been broken. I'm just trying to put all the pieces back together. Anyone who knows me knows that I have a very strong, confident, and deep personality. It's either black or white – no grey in between.

I speak my mind, and I always have, sometimes too much. It gets me into trouble. I just don't know when to shut up. Put it this way – you won't be left wondering what I was thinking by the end of a conversation with me. Some people like that; some people don't. At the end of the day, I don't really care. You either love me or you hate me. The majority of people love me, I hope.

My brain never switches off and it gets a bit carried away, making up little scenarios of every situation. You can be having a conversation with me, but at the same time my brain will be thinking about something else already.

I hold a grudge for a very long time. If you do the wrong thing by me, my friend Maree says I plot my revenge before the incident has even happened. Sad but true – she knows me better than most.

I don't apologise – or not very often anyway. Even if I am wrong, I won't admit it.

I have a very big circle of friends because of where I have grown up and worked over my life.

I swear. A lot. Sometimes I mean to; other times, it just rolls off the tongue naturally without me even realising I'm saying it.

I like to laugh and have fun, but I also like to cry; it lets you know that you're still human and still have a heart inside.

Most of the time you'll only get one chance with me, but for my true friends and family, I will love them fiercely till the end. I'm very loyal and a good friend to have on your side in a battle.

I also am very quick-tempered. I can go from 0 to 100 very quickly.

I have been told I have two spirits sitting on my shoulders: Charlie Angel on one side and Charlie Devil on the other. A lot of the time, Charlie Devil takes over without me even realising what's happening. This is when I get myself into trouble.

I have been told I have multiple personalities, which is true to a point. Once you read this book, you'll understand why I do. I have to protect myself and control all the different roles I have to play.

One of my worst traits is that my protective instinct pushes people away if they get too close. In the past, I have lost people that I wish I had not. But there is no point crying over spilt milk. What's done is done. Sometimes I wish I could go back and change those decisions, but I can't. So onwards and upwards. The world is still spinning and that's never going to change.

*****

So, happy reading. I hope you enjoy it and learn that when you think it's the end of the world, it's not: there is always a silver lining somewhere. Some days I wonder how, then it can change in the blink of an eye and suddenly… everything is all good again.

Part 1:
Growing Up As A Country Girl

Charlie prep photo

Charlie & Priest Father O'Toole

Chapter 1:
My Small-Town Country Upbringing

"Small town, big heart."
Phillip Aaberg

I was lucky enough to have grown up in a small country town called Lalbert, just about 50km out of Swan Hill, Victoria. I wouldn't have changed it for the world. It was a very small, tight-knit community surrounded by family and friends. There wasn't much you could do without anyone knowing your business. We didn't have to worry about hiding secrets from our parents for very long because the news got back to the them before we were even home. They used to call it the old Bush Telegraph: if you want someone to know something, just whisper in one person's ear and everyone else in the town will do the rest of the work for you. Honestly, it is a bit of a laugh, really.

We were made to go to church weekly. We had the early starts on Sunday mornings at 8.30am or 10.30am, then the 7.30pm of a Saturday night – which was a joke because footy had been all day already, then to the pub, then to church. The majority of the time, the priest ended up back at the pub with us!

My job in church with my cousins was to stand up the front and do the projector, which meant putting the songs up for everyone to sing. We had a running joke that there was one older lady that played the organ and really thought she could sing, but believe me, she could not! So we all used to sing at the top of our lungs to try and drown her out. How we laughed! The boys were the altar boys, so they had to put the robes on and carry out the candles, which I look back on now and find very comical.

As we got older, we did our communion and confirmation, which then meant we were allowed to receive weekly communion. For those of you who were not brought up catholic, it means halfway through the service you line up and receive a bit of bread, which they called the body of Christ – and we got to have a small sip of the wine. I remember they would break a bit of bread and drop it in the wine. One of my cousins and I used to try and gulp the wine to see if we could get the piece of bread as a bit of a game. I look back now and think… bloody hell! That was rank, but funny at the time.

I loved having such a big family. It's great. Christmas was always awesome: there was always someone to play with or fight with – which ever came first. When you have such a big family, it also means there's always someone who has your back and someone to love you no matter what. We were all extremely close and still are to this day, keeping in pretty great contact with each other. I suppose that's the beauty of modern technology with Facebook, Snapchat, Instagram, and everything else that can keep you in the loop. There's no excuse not to be these days.

I have two older brothers, Paul and Jamie, and a half-sister, Katrina. When growing up, sometimes they were good to me; sometimes they were mean. I guess that's just families – pick on the little sister or be the big protective brother in the pub for her, whichever comes first. Although admittedly, I didn't need much protecting. I was stubborn with a pretty sharp tongue and didn't take much crap from anyone. I was always ready to look after myself and that hasn't changed. A good friend once said, "Bloody hell, Charlie, it's either black or white with you and no grey in between." I still believe this to be true, and you usually only get one chance with me…

Because the town I grew up in was so small, we relied heavily on our sports and our local pub for community. That became our lives: getting up, ready to go to play tennis and cricket in the summer or netball and footy in the winter. Our sports were the highlight of our Saturdays. I love tennis. As juniors, we played in many premierships and then we were all taken up to play seniors quickly because of our numbers – but a lot of the time we kicked the arse of the adults anyway!

As much as I loved tennis, I loved netball more. It was my passion. I was super competitive, and I had white line fever. That meant I was friends with my friends before we took the court, but once on the court, we were enemies. My favourite position was goal attack (GA). I was quite a good little goalie, winning many best and fairest, including in the league when I was playing juniors, and then won best and fairest in the league in C grade years later, which was the best grade to play in to have fun. I played drunk a few times.

We never won many games, but back then we played for the love of the game. Although when we did happen to win a game, it was pretty special. Sally and I used to sneak over to the pub after we had played our junior game and have a pot of beer. They would serve us if we sat around the corner in the lounge! I also coached junior netball as well as umpiring.

A little club had a paper that came out about all the things that had happened during the week. I used to write a column called "Netball News with Charlie". I wrote up all the scores, all the votes, all the gossip, and all the news that had happened during the week whilst trying to study at school. One of my schoolteachers was the editor of this paper. His name was Mick McGowan, otherwise known as McGoo. He was forever chasing me for my article. I turned around and said to him one day, "Do you want me to do my schoolwork or do the article?" He just stared at me. I turned around, walked off, and laughed.

Our senior football was always very competitive as well. We won many premierships as a club, and this always called for a big celebration: the whole town gathered and basically stopped for a week. When we were in the grand final, we always dressed up in our footy colours. I have a photo of my me and my cousin, Lee. We were completely covered in all our colours, blue and gold from top to bottom. We actually got our photo in the paper that year. Sport was what kept our community together, and it was a wonderful thing.

I went to a little school. It consisted of about 30 children and two classrooms. In my grade, there was only five of us: myself, Stacey, Lee, Simon, and Duane, who I still have contact with now. Stacey and I, being the only girls, were close, and we are still good friends to this day. I have fun memories of these days.

The name of one of my teachers was Miss Snelders. When we were naughty, she would make us sit against the cupboard with our nose on it. We would sit there and breathe on it and draw in it with our fingers. Needless to say, I spent a fair bit of time with my nose against the door. I sat next to my cousin Lee a lot. His nickname is Kermie. This came about later on – don't ask me how or why! But we were joined at the hip; being cousins, we had to stick together.

There wasn't much in our little school: a couple of shelter sheds, which I think I may have had my first kiss behind! There was an oval for us to play on and I do remember when a new big brick wall got put up so we could actually bounce balls against it. We all thought this was amazing.

Our athletics days in primary school were a huge deal. This was when we were given a scorecard – 1, 2, or 3 – on how we had faired in that event. These were also the days when they would make you sit behind which number you had got. That was before anyone had feelings to be hurt, but it was also pretty simple: you were either good at it or not. We weren't wrapped up in cotton wool then.

I was lucky enough during that part of my life to be able to run and jump, which I absolutely loved. I was good at it for a short while until I got to high school and snapped my anterior cruciate ligament running a 100m sprint. That was my first reconstruction at 16 – on my knee. This is why I encourage everyone to enjoy every possible thing that they can while they can because no one can see around corners, and no one knows what is in store for us in the future.

We also had a little store that sold hot chips, lollies, icy poles, and drinks. We would all jump off at the bus stop and try and get something before we had to make the next stage of our trip home. I had to travel an hour to school and an hour home by bus, then half an hour in the car to get home. The shop had a post office in it as well, so we could collect our mail. We had a garage with mechanics and we also had the local town pub which was the highlight for the whole community. We would all gather here after football, netball, and tennis, so everyone could have their drinks and tea for the evening, with us kids falling asleep underneath the tables before heading home.

I have so many amazing memories of that town, I can't even begin to say. There was so much more involved, I guess you just had to live there at the time. Unfortunately, there is not much left of it today except for the football club. The pub fell down, the shop is closed, and the hall got pulled down, so there is not much left in our little town.

Lalbert Pub

Charlie & Sally

My Small-Town Country Upbringing

Charlie on farm motorbike

Cousin family photo

Brother Paul, Charlie & brother Jamie

Maree, Kermie & Charlie

My Small-Town Country Upbringing

Page 4.   The Eagle Eye - No 1.   Thrs, 5th April, 1995.

OTHER NEWS

From Page 1...

saw as playing well before injured.

Lalbert played the match without numerous players available but the match gave the coach and selectors the opportunity to look at other players. What has been most pleasing is the form and improvement of a number of 1994 reserve players. One has to suspect that it has been due to pre season training and one hopes that they can get some reward for thier efforts with some wins and an opportunity to play seniors.

Another promising aspect has been the form of some young players namely Lee O'Meara, Jeremy Jones, Noval Evans, Tony Weir, Peter Johnson Terry Nancarrow and Paul O'Bree.

Having had three practice matches and recruited some promising players the Lalbert supporters look forward to a successful year. The netballers also have done some recruiting and it is hope that they to have a successful year. All the best to all players and supporters for the 95 season - from the girls who know football, netball and have a eye for talent.

SPECIAL THANKS

Special thanks are extended to all who participated in the working Bee at the Football grounds to prepare the place for the start to the season.

NETBALL NEWS
with
CHARLIE

Well... I'm back for season 1995, and hopefully, this year will be quite a successful year.

I give a big welcome to all the new recruits who have decided to play for the Eagles, and I'm sure you'll be guaranteed a good netball year and don't forget the Social Scene either!

I also congratulate Cathy Parkinson for accepting the coaching position of the A and B grade sides for this year, and hopefully Cathy will coach them through to the finals.

I know I'm speaking with confidence... but the only way to WIN is with confidence! So... come on girls, and we'll send those Roos home from their first match with their tails between their legs.

Kathy Alexander is taking care of the C grade side, and so far the team is looking very promising.

The Junior sides are in good form also with a few new players joining the side, and they are too are feeling optimistic.

Jenny Davies has decided to coach the 13 and under girls, while I am coaching the 17 and under and 15 and unders for the time being, until the sides have been confirmed.

So... that's all the Netball News, but if anyone wishes to contact me in strict confidence about some stories about Netballers, I would greatly appreciate it! Don't worry... you're secrets are safe with me!!! I'll be on the lookout for any embarrassing or humiliating stories!

And now for a few words about the Lalbert Tennis teams...

This year there were an A and B grade side with Juniors. Three out of the four teams made it into the Grand Final. The B grade Juniors missing out, even though they made it to the first final!

The B grade Seniors romped it in, not having hardly a worry all day, that they would bring the trophy home again.

It was a bit of a different story with the A grade sides. The Juniors were up by one going into the last set and won it 6/5 to give them victory by 2 games.

It was different for the Seniors, we were 1 down facing the mixed. Although we were confident with our mixed pairs, we knew anything could happen. But we won by 6 games and made history at the same time.

The last time A grade Seniors won the Grand Final was in **1926**... 70 years almost! How long? Too long anyway, so now all the trophies are hanging in the pub... at least that way everyone will see them!

That's enough from me for now... and Netballers don't forget to dob your best friend in when she does something stupid; that way everyone can share the humour!

See Ya,

CHARLIE

OTHER EFFORTS ACKNOWLEDGED

The LFC/MMFL Calendars come out in the Guardian of Friday 7th April. Appreciation is extended to Chris and Bernadette Warburton and their helpers who spent all of last Sunday sticking the Magnets on these Calendars.

Also, thanks to Gordie Mac for the large sign greeting all who enter the grounds!

LALBERT GARAGE
MAIN STREET,
LALBERT.
for all types of Automotive repairs.
AGENTS FORBOORT
TYRE SERVICE.
Telephone:
Beddgie or Gomer
(054) 573205

G. & J. McFARLANE
STOCK AGENTS
Agents for
Mobil
Lalbert
Telephone
(054) 57 3204

LALBERT RURAL FIRE BRIGADE

ANNUAL MEETING

Monday, 10th April
7:30 PM
at
the Shed
and at
the PUB
later
for the
Meeting

Local footy club newsletter Eagle Eye

Charlie & Sally bogging ute

Kp & Charlie

Chapter 2:
Getting Into Trouble As A Teenager

"We didn't realise we were making memories, we just knew we were having fun."

A A Milne, Winnie The Pooh

I started smoking when I was 13. My best friend Sally and I would go behind the church of all places. I bet my mum doesn't know that. We used to go off and do all lots of sneaky things. We used to pinch a few beers out of Sally's Mum and Dad's cool room, and we thought they didn't know this whole time. We used to just grab a couple of stubbies out and then we would jump in her dad's ute, drive up the railway line and drink them. We got the Ute bogged once, then covered ourselves in mud, so at least it looked like we had attempted to get it out.

We thought we were living the best life. We found Sally's mum's old joint in her drawer one day and we smoked that too. I only found out recently, but she actually knew that we had done that. Sally and I spent all our time together, drinking and smoking in Sal's dad's shed. We used to drink VB and smoke menthols back then. I practically spent every weekend at the McFarlanes. I was close to the whole family: Janine, Gordon, Clinton, and Leanne. Even when I was older, I moved in with them.

My teenage years I also remember very fondly. We grew up on a farm, raising and bottle-feeding newborn calves. My brothers used to call me spoilt because I got to get out of mowing the lawns and doing most of

Fierce and Unstoppable

Charlie & Marnie

the other stuff around the farm while they had to do all the work. I got to play with my netball ring, lie on my trampoline, play on the slide, and I had a cubby house where I used to go and hide away from everyone.

Mum used to kill the chooks, boil them up in the boiler, and then we would have to pluck them and then eat them. They were disgusting. My mum worked hard. She used to go out weeding tomatoes in the middle of summer just to make extra money to buy us kids Christmas presents. I do appreciate what mum did for us.

I remember one day being out in the paddock with my brother Jamie and we had two golf sticks – one each. We were hitting dry cow pads, and as he hit one, it was soft in the middle, and he covered me in wet cow shit. My temper got the better of me. I cracked it. I turned around and whacked him fair in the ankle with the golf stick and dropped him to the ground. He started yelling out and crying for mum, so I ran for the hills and hid until teatime. I knew I had to go home but the

Getting Into Trouble As A Teenager

Marnie, Charlie & Melissa

outcome was still going to be the same: a good kick in the arse. It was worth it, though. I still don't think I've laughed so hard since I did that. At least he got a sore ankle out of it considering I was covered in shit. I was closer to my older brother, Paul. He used to take me out shooting and looked after me. Poor Jamie had the middle-child syndrome.

There were a lot of memorable times and the majority of them involved alcohol and our local pub. It was a small town, not much else to do. While our parents were at the pub, they gave us our six-pack to head down to the old dam and light a fire. We weren't hurting anyone.

This night was my cousin's 18th birthday. I was 15, but I was sneaking beer the whole night. I was going on great until the drive home and then I started to feel sick. I had my brother, my mum, my stepfather, and my cousin all in the car. I started to feel ill. I put the window down to try and get some fresh air to make me feel a little bit better. As we dropped my cousin home, he opened the door, and the fresh air came in. I thought, "Thank God, I'm going to be okay." But no.

Charlie & Marnie 15th bday in barn Charlie Lalbert

As we got up the road a little bit further, I couldn't hold it in any longer. It came out of me like a fountain. I managed to vomit all over my brother, my mum – in the front, my stepfather – driving, and I got the roof of the car as well. My punishment the next day was to go out and clean up all the vomit. I thought I was going to do it all over again. There is nothing quite like the smell of vomit in the morning, and I'm sure my mother is still laughing about that till this day.

My first day of high school was a big deal. Coming from a school of 30 kids to an enormous, sprawling place was very daunting. We had an assembly with the principal, Mr Rush, who was very intimidating to say the least. We were then put into our classrooms, and this short little girl, who wore glasses and a Coca Cola bag on

Getting Into Trouble As A Teenager

Charlie

her back, introduced herself to me. Her name was Carmel, and I was so appreciative of her that day. Once again, she still remains an important part of my life.

My girlfriends used to come out for my birthday parties. My 13th birthday party was particularly memorable. We had all been storing and sneaking alcohol from our parents, grandparents – wherever we could get hold of it. My friend Chelsea stored hers in sauce bottles, brought it to school in our bags, and took it home to my place ready to have a few drinks that night. We were all just sitting around together talking and laughing when Mum walked in. "How are you, girls?" We all replied, "Great, thanks."

She then said, "Would you like to put your grog in the fridge?" We all just looked at each other in shock. She went on, "I didn't come down in the last shower, you know, but you better put that grog in the fridge. There is no point drinking it hot. It'll make you crook." It was that day I realised that my mum was actually pretty cool.

Melissa, Lee, Charlie, Chels
Charlie 10 tequila shots 15th birthday

My next birthday party would've been my 15th. We had an old barn, so once again, we all gathered up our alcohol, but this time we stepped it up a notch – we had bought a bottle of tequila. I'm not sure who from; I would imagine one of the older cousins. So there we were, a bunch of 15-year-old girls dancing around in the barn, drinking tequila shots from the bottle with the red Mexican hat. I'm sure the girls can still remember this day, and tequila is still my favourite poison – lip, sip, suck.

Another time when the girls come to stay, my brother Paul lit a bonfire down the paddock for us, but this time for the alcohol, we had Blackberry Nip and a bottle of Stones. I don't know where we

Getting Into Trouble As A Teenager

Charlie's 15th birthday

got our hands on it – probably from Paul, but it was bloody terrible. Anyway, we still danced and drank away around the fire and had another good time.

Golf was also a huge part of our upbringing. Our parents used to play golf and so did we, every Sunday. All us kids of a night would run around the fairways playing British bulldogs a game you would run and then get tackled. As we got older, the boys would play a game where they rolled up a piece of paper, stick it in their bum cheeks, light it, and then run as fast as they could before it burnt them – this was hilarious to watch!

Every year, there was a golf day called Macca's golf day which was organised by Sally's dad. He was a promoter. There was this one hole, the tip hole, where they set up a bar. Sally and I served all the alcohol to the male golfers as they were going around. We would've been all of 15, but I'm pretty sure that we were drunker than what they were by the end of the day!

I spent a lot of time at Sally's. We smoked and drank in her dad's shed. I know that seems terrible. Looking back, that's all we seemed to do, but when you grow up in a small town, there's not much else to do. I also remember at her 13th birthday when we went to the pub and bought our first slab of beer – Fosters lager in the blue can. We went and stayed in one of their old houses in town with all the girls, but I'm pretty sure the boys found us too.

Mum had never let me shave my legs until that point, so we had razors. We probably took them from Sal's mum, and we shaved my legs. I still remember going home and telling mum about my legs. She wasn't happy about it at all because, "Now you have to keep shaving them. You can't just leave them alone now." I can still hear her voice in my head.

My high school years were fantastic. I made some of the best friends for life and I still have them now. When we ring, we talk as if we only spoke yesterday, when really it could have been a year.

Once we hit high school, the Deb balls started too. All my friends did their Deb in Swan Hill. I did mine out at Lalbert in the hall. There was only five of us girls in that one because there hadn't been a debutante ball there in 30 years! It was a highlight of the town when our Deb ball took place. I did my Deb with Simon Schlitz. He was a local Quamby boy who I'd been friends with for a long time by that point. We played a lot of tennis together too. I think I actually had a crush on him at some point in time.

There were plenty of balls in Swan Hill as well. I remember one night, us girls got the courage to walk from the hall to the pub. We snuck in the back. We thought we were so cool. Then, to my shock, my big

Chels, Charlie. Marn & Renee Lalbert Deb

Charlie Lalbert Deb ball

Charlie & Carms Deb ball   *Charlie & Evo*

brother Paul was standing there. He was an actual pain. I couldn't move without him following me. If I needed to go to the toilet, he would follow me. He got me a drink then. He stood there while I drank it – for the whole time – to make sure that no one came near me. I don't think he could bear the thought that his little sister was actually growing up.

These were fun times. I would do anything to turn the clock back, to be able to be there for just a second and relive those moments. Big parts of my high school years were spent with my best friends Marnie and Chelsea. There were so many others as well – I can't even name them all, but we are all still good friends today.

One memory that comes to mind was when I was staying at Marnie's house. Her parents had gone to Queensland and left us home alone. They had bought a small bottle of Southern Comfort for us while they were gone, but of course, we got Marnie's big brother Brock to go and buy us a big 750ml bottle as well. For some unknown reason, we decided to do it in shots. Why we wouldn't have mixed it with Coke, I have no clue. Anyway, Marnie ended up spewing all through her bed while I at least made it to the toilet. Still to this day, I cannot stand smell of Southern Comfort.

High school years are honestly the best times of our lives; it sets the foundation for your future. My mother always told me school is the best time of your life. I never believed her until I finally had to get a job and support myself. Although, in saying that, every time I did go home to the farm, my car magically found itself parked right beside the fuel bowser... thanks Mum and Bill!

After year 12, we used to spend a lot of time at the pub. We practically ran the pub. We made our own drinks; Illusions were our specialty. Then we would get up and dance on the bar. Not much was remembered for the rest of the night after that stage. One time our biggest brain waves was we would go out, get in our cars, and do circle work at the front of the silos, come back, have a beer and then repeat. It was a lot of fun. As I said, it was a small town and there wasn't much else to do.

At that time, I was living in Lalbert with my boyfriend Drew. I moved out of home at 17. We had known each other all our lives as we all had grown up together. We spent a lot of time out at the lake as he owned a ski boat. That was how our relationship started: me prancing around in my bikinis as you do at that age: if you've got it flaunt it because believe me, that body doesn't stay like that forever – gravity takes over!

One thing turned into another, and next thing you know, we were boyfriend and girlfriend and living together. He was the same age as my eldest brother Paul, which Mum wasn't very happy about to start with, but eventually she got used to the idea. Well, she didn't really have a choice! He was my first serious boyfriend after finishing year 12. It lasted a couple of years, but of course, as per usual, it ended in heartbreak and hate. It wasn't a nice breakup, but when are they ever a good time?

At that age, a breakup feels like your world is ending and there is nothing left to look forward to. Young love, eh? Well, we all know this is just a temporary thing. Although, mine lasted – not speaking to him for nearly 20 years. That was all on my behalf because I am a stubborn bitch and hold a grudge for a long time. He did try to talk to me, but I just didn't want to hear it. (They do say the best way to get over one is to get under another. I didn't do this. Maybe I should have? Just food for thought…)

I did work while I lived in Lalbert. I was a perfume consultant. People would hold parties in their house and you would sell perfume to them. Believe it or not, there is actually good money in perfume parties if you do it right. I was lucky enough to have the gift of the gab and could talk people into nearly anything.

I drove the versatile tractor on the family farm, though one day I managed to wipe out one of the paddock's fences. I didn't do this job for very long. Eggy, my uncle, took me to the Culgoa pub instead, and we came home rolling drunk.

I also worked on the local weighbridge over harvest. I actually had to work while my friends went away for schoolies week after we finished year 12. I had originally planned to go. I booked my ticket and everything, but work came first, and I needed the money so I could buy my first car. One day working on the weighbridge, I went flying over to the bunkers, lost it in the loose wheat on the road, and hit a post.

I came back most upset, so my boss, Barry Kelly, who was super cool, went over to the pub and bought me a can of brandy, lime, and soda to calm me down. Barry was a great boss. He smoked like a trooper in the weighbridge, even though he wasn't allowed, so we had to try and have a clean-up when the grain elevator's board workers were coming. Barry was very overweight, so his wife would make him salad sandwiches. He would go and throw these to the birds, then go over to the shop and buy a couple of pies. I laughed, but I was sworn to secrecy...

I was still working the weighbridge the night of my 18th birthday because harvest doesn't stop. You started about 7am in the morning and finished at 7pm at night – or whenever the last truck comes through. Therefore, everyone was turning up to the pub while I was still working, but they still came over and had drinks with me in the weighbridge while I worked because it was directly opposite the pub, and that's where my party was. I know it sounds like I had a lot of birthday parties, which I did, because I love them: I love being around people, my friends, and family, so I will continue to have parties as for as long as I can.

After the year 1995, everyone had started to make their own ways. By now most people were all off at uni. I went to Bendigo uni. I had applied at Warrnambool to do public relations, but I missed the first-round offers. I was offered a spot at Bendigo for a Bachelor of Arts, which is a bullshit course – basically you do whatever you like! I was studying politics. I was devastated because second-round offers came out and I was offered the course that I wanted, but it was too late. I'd already accepted to go to Bendigo.

I went off to uni for a little while, though it didn't last because I thought I was in love, so I left and came home. I did move into town after that breakup and rented a two-bedroom flat with Kermie for a little while before I pissed off to Queensland. I just had to get out of town.

I lived in Queensland for a short while. I couldn't get work much when I was there. I considered becoming a promo girl at one of the night clubs, which would have been better than what I ended up doing. I actually started selling Kirby vacuums, which was a very hard task. One night on my drive home after a presentation, I wasn't concentrating. I didn't give way at an intersection and hit another car. I wrote my car off, not long after that, I got sick and ended up in hospital with pneumonia and had to come home. Instead of flying home, Mum made me come home on the bus – what a bloody experience that was and a very long trip!

I still regret leaving my younger cousin, Maree, behind, but I had no choice. I just had to go. She will never forgive me because she was pregnant at the time and I just left her, breaking my heart. Maree was my closest little cousin. I had dragged her around with me from party to party, place to place since she was 14. How the hell Aunty Lila let me actually take her, I don't know. But I didn't do a very good job of looking after her because she got bloody pregnant. Out of every situation, we have to hope for the best.

We were given a beautiful little girl, Paige, who has turned into to one of the most kind and loving young girls I know. The year that Maree got pregnant I was coaching the netball team. I don't know what I did wrong, but instead of giving them PONSTAN for period pain, I should've been giving them the pill – because three of the girls ended up pregnant. I had some answering to do. Once I took them on a netball trip to Kangaroo Lake Caravan Park. My dad drove the bus and, yes, I got them all drunk. Great influence I was.

We went on a lot of netball trips as we got older which were just piss trips and having fun. One year, our bus broke down and we were stranded on the road outside of St Arnaud. We were on our way to Ballarat – luckily our esky was full!

Now that I was back home, I was heavily involved in sports again with the football club, playing netball, coaching, umpiring, drinking, having a great time with KP – another one of my great friends; it was like you see one, you see the other. We used to write letters to each other, and she kept them all. We had a great time reliving these and laughing about all our fun together and all the old boyfriends. Bloody hell! And how we became the talk of the town – got to love small-town gossip… or was it?

We were just having fun. In one of the letters, it talks about how Mum tried to sit me down and told me that I needed to control my drinking. I was 16. She told me I get loose and out of control. Well, not much has changed, so that chat obviously didn't work!

Our club that we played netball and football for was Lalbert in the Mid Murray league. It was considered the major league. I always joke with a friend that he was from Ultima, and they were in the minor-league, so we were above and better than them. He used to call us stuck-up, isn't that right Darren? Maree said we weren't stuck up but just cool and better than them!

KP and I used to alternate our time between the local footy sheds and the local pub, and then into Swan Hill to hang out with the boys to get into the Oasis, the nightclub at the time.

Sometimes I look back and I'm not entirely proud of some of the decisions I had made, but then, it wasn't me who was the guilty one. We all go through this stage of our lives where we go to the pubs, we pick up and have one-night-stands to get up the next day and think, *What the fuck have I done?*

Thinking back now, I do feel sorry for one bloke I took home. I thought he was okay in the pub, but I got home and thought, *Oh my God, how am I going to get out of this?* I tried every excuse under the sun – that I had my period; that my brothers were going to turn up. Nothing worked, so I ended up getting up, getting dressed, and going back to the pub, then asked him to leave. Poor bastard. Thought he had scored for the night…

Sally & Charlie

Lee, Marn, Charlie & Penny

Getting Into Trouble As A Teenager

Charlie & Evo

Maree & Charlie

Fierce and Unstoppable

Chels.Charlie Marn, Lee & Penny

Chels & Charlie

Mick & Charlie at 16th

Carms & Charlie at 16th

Chapter 3:
My Sweet 16

"Dance like no one is watching, love like you've never been hurt; sing like no one is listening and live like it's heaven on Earth."

William Watson Purkey

My 16th, which I held with my best friend Sally, was in an old paddock just outside of Lalbert. One of the old farmers had let us light a great big bonfire there. This time was really the big party. We brought out a bus of kids, full of teenagers ranging from probably 14 to almost 16. My old bus driver Johnny Curthoys had agreed to pick the kids up in town and drive them all out. They stayed there till midnight then he came and picked them up and took them home.

What everyone told their parents – whether they were coming out for that party or whether they were allowed to or not – I'm not sure. Once again, because I had so many cousins and friends, all the older kids were waiting in town for us to come off the bus. They came out in utes picked us all up. We jumped in the back, and they drove us into Lalbert to the pub to buy our alcohol, and then we went back out to the paddock for the mother of all parties!

We all drank straight spirits because for some stupid reason we weren't smart enough to carry soft drink to mix it with. I'm sure you can imagine not all of it was kept in our stomachs. I still can feel the excitement and happy vibes of that night. It is still talked about fondly by everyone who attended that night – never to be forgotten. It was the night of our lives: a real, true country-town party with the fire going, music, dancing, and plenty of hookups happened that night.

It really was the best party of our life and will still be talked about at our school reunions we go to, I'm sure. A lot of the parents would've had no idea where their kids were going that night, or if they did, and let their kids go on a bus trip to bonfire in the middle of paddock full of young kids and alcohol, they were pretty laid-back.

In all honesty, we weren't hurting anyone. We were out in the middle of nowhere, just having a good time and enjoying life as young kids should do. I feel sorry for the kids today because they don't get to live the life that we did: with freedom and no one looking over your shoulder every five minutes. We used to be able to ride bikes with no helmet and get away with almost anything. But now, they're watched by everyone, and with social media and smartphones, you can't get away with a single thing.

All I can say is thank God there were no phones back in our day for everyone to be recorded. Bloody hell! I'm worried about what my children are reading now. Imagine if they'd seen what we've done, and it had been recorded back then? I know this sounds like we drank a lot, which we probably did, but there was nothing else for us to do…

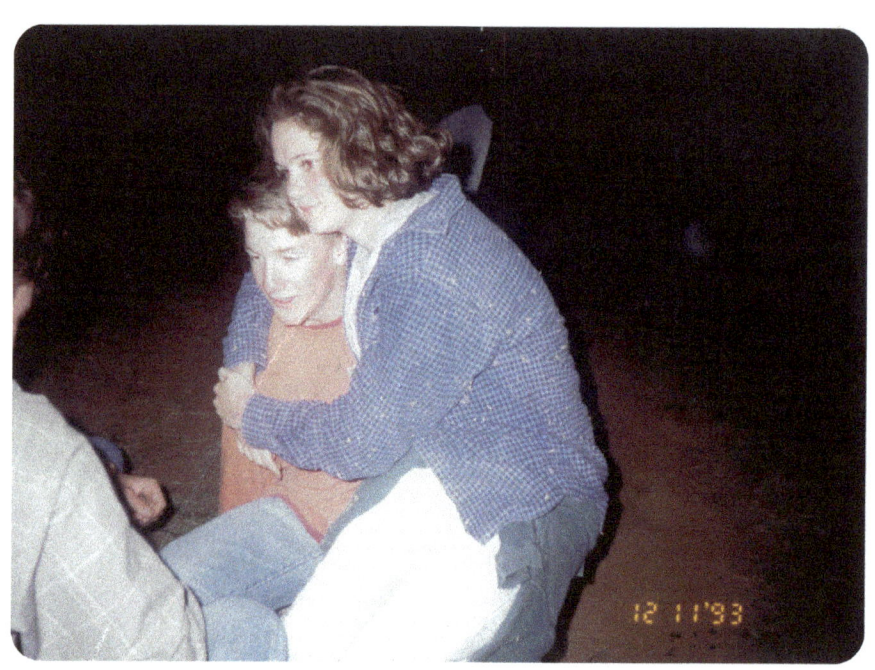

Marcus & Charlie

Chapter 4:
Losing My Virginity

"It takes courage to grow up and become who you really are."
E.E. Cummings

The majority of us had boyfriends at the time. My boyfriend's name was Marcus. I had a bet with my oldest brother Paul that I wouldn't lose my virginity before I was 16. I had a week to go, so, no, I didn't win the bet. If you can imagine being a young 15-year-old girl, with your boyfriend there with you – it was dark; everyone was drinking and drunk around the fire.

We snuck off. I put my flannel shirt on the ground and lay down. I was so nervous and scared. I had no idea what to expect. All the other bases had been covered except for the last one… So we took the final step. Fuck me: it burnt and stung like a bitch! Believe me, girls, don't expect or believe what you see on the movies because if anyone says their first time was a special and enjoyable time – they are fucking lying.

I'm assuming for the boys it probably does blow their mind and feel like stars are shooting out of their arse, but for us poor girls? Well, all I can say is that it does get better with time. So the deed was done, tick that off the bucket list that can never be returned… We went back to the fire. I sat on his knee with my flannel back on, with a back full of grass seeds – which was a dead giveaway to everyone what we had been up to! We all still laugh about the grass seeds, especially Carmel.

So the party went on; we kept drinking, smoking, and enjoying the party. I still think Marcus and I were pretty proud of ourselves. I'm also pretty sure we weren't the only ones who lost the big V that night! To this day, every time I drive past that paddock, I look in and smile because you never forget your first.

Talking about driving past – I was with friends going away for the weekend to Stawell and we drove past the paddock. As we went past, I yelled out to all of them, "I lost my virginity in that paddock!" Everyone on the bus burst out laughing. We still talk about it to this day. It's hilarious. I can feel my kids cringing right now, but if they're reading this, I think it's funny. It's part of life.

That's how we make memories, and doing this would have to be one of the most important memories of your life because once you lose it, it's never coming back. We were always told that losing your virginity should be to someone special but honestly, it doesn't matter. It's just another milestone in that has to happen at some stage during your life. I guess at least I can remember it and laugh about how it happened. It was a memorable moment that I will never forget and neither will a lot of others.

We broke up not long after this night. Young love, eh? I guess it just wasn't meant to be! I don't think I was even too worried about the whole thing: move on to greener pastures and so on. Years later, I saw him in the pub with his mates, and I walked past. I was going to say hi, but I heard him bragging to his mates, "Oh, I broke her in." He was really carrying on, so I spun around and said, "Yes, he did. But do you want to know what, boys? He has the smallest dick I have ever seen and was the worst lay of my life." All his mates made fun of him while I went off laughing. I thought, *That will teach you smart-arse – all you had to do was say hello!*

Robyn, Shelley, Sonia. Charlie, Kymm, Carms

Charlie & Marn

Chapter 5:
My Lifelong Best Friends

"A real friend is one who walks in when the rest of the world walks out."
Walter Winchell

We had a school reunion where I went with my oldest friends and caught up with all the kids who went to school with. It's funny after a few drinks – you find out what people really thought about you in school. Marnie and I got the shock of our lives. We didn't realise that people had actually felt intimidated by us in school. We thought we were just everyone's friend. I had one of the boys, who I'm friends with, tell me that he actually was scared of me in school. I still couldn't believe it. I was in shock! We had a really good laugh about it and then went on to have a very good night.

There are friends, but then there are best friends. Mine were Marnie, Chels, and Sonia. These are the ones who hold all the secrets, tell you the truth, and who you pick up the phone and call. We also had a small group of friends which consisted of Marnie, Chels, Pen, Lee, Melissa, Monika, and Donna. Marn and I probably paired off quite a bit. This was the group that was our daily group that we hung out with before school, recess, and lunch time. I have spent a lot of time with these girls together and separately. I spent a lot of my high school times with Marnie at her house with herself and her family, who I am still close with.

Marn and I used to wag school go back to her house and sunbake for the day. As we were walking back to school, we were having a smoke and her dad drove past. We quickly dropped it, praying he hadn't seen

Charlie & KP

us, so that became one of our jokes between us – "Quick, drop it, Nev –" and laughed every time.

Another time after we finished year 12, we all went camping out at Lake Boga. I had my licence by that point, so that gave us some freedom. One of the days we were out there, Marn and I got in floating tubes and sat in the sun all day. We didn't think we were getting burnt because we kept splashing water on ourselves to cool us down, but bloody hell, when we got out, we looked like lobsters and blistered almost instantly. A word of advice – do not do this. We whinged and bitched about it for days. I still remember how much that hurt. When Marnie got her first car, it was a yellow Torana. We used to call him Tommy; we had a lot of fun in this car.

Our group consisted of both boys and girls; we hung out mainly with the Piangil boys. We used to camp on the Elford's Farm which involved

My Lifelong Best Friends

Charlie & Penny

more drinking, smoking, and motorbikes. Once, Joel and I were on one of the bikes, went over a jump, and both fell off. Neither of us had helmets on. It was surprising, but neither of us hurt ourselves. How our parents let us go, I'm still dumbfounded: young boys and girls sleeping out together in an old farmhouse. I was going out with Timmy Frost at the time. He was such a hotty and a sweetheart. Our parents were all pretty cool and obviously very trusting. Maybe if they are reading this, they may have done things differently!

One night, the boys rolled up some parsley in papers and handed it to one of the older boys. He smoked it thinking it was a joint. Next thing, he thought he was stoned. We were all rolling around in laughter because we all knew it was only parsley.

When we stayed at Chelsea's, we used to sneak out and go up to the railway line to meet the boys. They all used to walk from town; it was

Fierce and Unstoppable

Charlie, Lee, Chon. Marn. Josh & Melissa

a few kilometres away. Amazing what teenage hormones can do… It always involved drinking, smoking, and, of course, hookups. These were the days, just praying Chels's parents didn't wake up and find us gone. Although they probably knew anyway. Back then, we did a lot of walking into town or around the town as we didn't drive.

It's funny how life takes us in different directions. Once I moved in with Brian, we lived just up the road from Chels's family home, so when she came home from uni, it was fate we were back together again.

I nearly forgot about this night until Marn showed me a photo. We all gathered at Marnie's house to have a few drinks, all turning up in similar outfits without planning it. We had our drinks then decided to go out. We were 16 at the time, made our way into the pub, and in doing so, we caught up with some AFL Richmond footballers that were in town. They were kind enough to walk us home, but we weren't silly. They were men after all if you get my drift!

My Lifelong Best Friends

Marn & Charlie

We were going back to Lee's place, but I stopped with one of them before we got there, and well, let your imagination do the rest… Get your mind out of the gutter! It was just a kiss and a bit of mucking around. When I got back to Lee's, I had a big smile on my face, so they knew what had happened. But typically, as girls do, they wanted to know every detail.

Funnily enough, probably about a year later, I was at a wedding with a friend and his brother had been a former Richmond footballer, so he was there. I nearly died looking at him, thinking there was no way he would remember me. I was wrong. He did, came over, and asked me for a dance. I probably hadn't changed much apart from filling out a bit more in the right places. After the reception ended, a few of us went back to the motel rooms we were staying at, and, yes, kissed him once again. Well, that is my claim to fame! Probably not a great one, but I will take it.

Chels came to stay out at Lalbert one day. Bill, my stepfather, had us going out with him while their crops were being sprayed. We had to stand up each end of the paddock and wave the white flags for the plane as he went past and then change ends. After we had finished, Bill took us to the pub and got us drunk. I still remember looking around the pub for Chelsea and I couldn't find her, so I walked outside to find her passed out in the grass just beside the pub.

Chelsea went through a vegetarian stage where she wouldn't eat any meat whatsoever. She got to the stage where she nearly drove us crazy because she wouldn't even eat chicken chips because they had animal fat in them. She's going to kill me for writing this book, but I always remind her every time. When we used to come out of the Oasis at the end of the night, which was the local nightclub, there was always a hotdog van waiting for us, and because we'd been drinking all night, we always were starving. I lined up to get my hotdog just about ready to bite into it and then Chelsea came along, took it out of my hands and ate it. I just stared at her and said, "Well, fucking hell. I take it you're not a vegetarian anymore!" This was just one of many nights that we had spent together out at the pubs, enjoying each other's company.

My time with Sonia, well, I spent a lot of time with her in and after high school. I was a bit of a floater in high school. I did float from group to group, but they were all still my really good friends, so I enjoyed it. Sonia was part of a lot bigger group than my other one, but it was still a lot of fun. We still used to go out together a lot as well. Kymm, Carmel, Narelle, Rosa, and Shelley were all part of this group; they, too, were part of my very large circle of friends.

Once again, our time together included a lot of drinking, camping, and parties. I was lucky our groups combined together at parties. They were part of the Wipeout time, which was the cheap version of Malibu. There was also blue curaçao, which we drank in abundance at one of Ral's parties and I spewed my guts up!

Marn. Charlie & Penny

Charlie & Chels

Cheryl, Trakka, Charlie & Caz

My Lifelong Best Friends

Chels, Charlie & Marn

Marn & Charlie

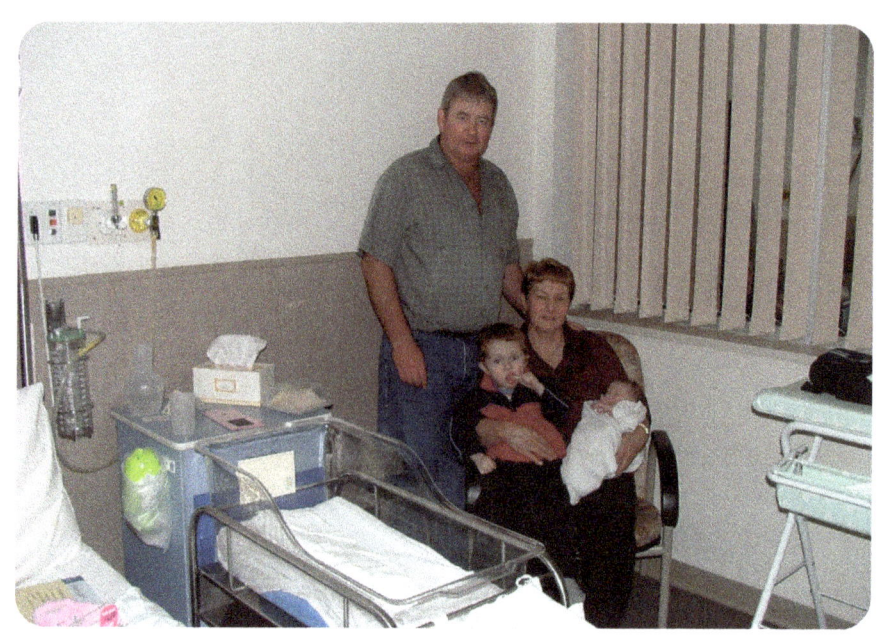

Bill, Shirley (mum) Josh & Hayley

Chapter 6:
My Busy Family Life

"The strength of a family, like the strength of an army, is in its loyalty to each other."

Mario Puzo

I am one of four: I have two brothers, Paul and Jamie, then a half-sister Katrina because when dad remarried, he had another daughter. My mum also remarried and stayed married for a further 36 years until Bill passed away in 2024. Bill was a big part of our life and practically raised us. He used to run me around to all my sport and to Melbourne to all my specialists for my sporting injuries. He loved us kids like his own.

My family was huge. My mum's sister moved to Lalbert first, then the other two sisters followed, and along came the family afterwards. Just to give you a little bit of an insight as to the size of my family, my mum was one of six, Charles (deceased), Lila dec, Ken, Shirley, Yvonne, and Sylvia Dec Jones. My great grandmother on mum's side was German and couldn't speak a word of English, maybe that's where my temper originates from! My dad was one of ten: Jack dec, Margaret dec, Carmel dec, Noreen, Brendan, Raymond (Sam), Pauline, Dorothy, Patricia, and Julie. You can imagine the number of cousins that came from all of that.

On my mum's side, there was 20 cousins: Aunty Lila had nine of her own. Then on my dad's side, there was another 27 cousins, so in total, that meant 47 cousins just in one family. There obviously wasn't any

Josh & Hayley

TV back in those days, not much else for us to do. I will leave it to your imagination! Your mind can only boggle at the next lot of generation coming through and how many of us there are now. That is why you never talk about anyone in a small town because everyone's related somewhere along the line.

We always called, and still do, all of our aunts and uncles with "Aunt" or "Uncle" in front of their name as it was what we were taught to say. For instance, Lila was called Aunty Lila – in actual fact, if we didn't address her that way, we nearly got a kick in the bum. It was like a respect thing, or they just liked the idea that we belonged to them. I do the same with my nieces and nephews, plus all of mine give me a hug when they see me. That is just the rules. Even all my cousins, where I am close with their kids, call me Aunty Charlie. Also, a lot of my close friends' kids and their kids call me by that too, which I just absolutely love. It warms my heart every time.

My Busy Family Life

Brian, Hayley & Josh

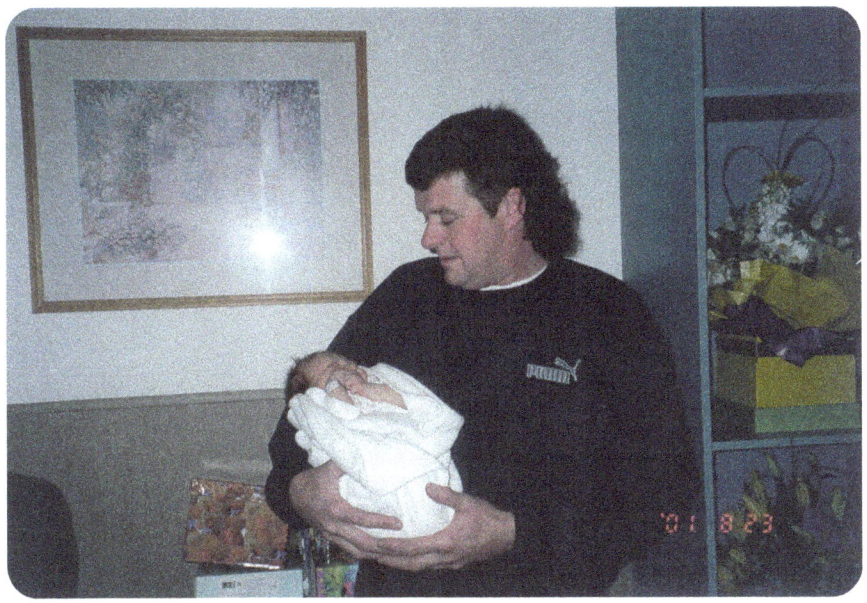

Brian & Josh

Brian & Josh

You were all probably having a little laugh to yourself by now and realising that, yes, we were Catholics – breeding like rabbits and multiplying. We were made to go to church every week until we turned 18, and then we could make up our own mind. Yes, I know, I know. Can you believe it or not? Yes, I did.

I just want to quickly write about our beloved cousin Cheryl. She was the matriarch of all the cousins. But I write this while having tears in my eyes because she passed away, 20 years ago now, with breast cancer, and left behind three little kids and a husband. We all still miss her dearly.

I spent most of my life with my cousins on my mum's side because we used to live just up the road from them. We would run to each other's houses. It was only a couple kilometres. I still remember Aunty Lila yelling at us. This is why Maree, Kermie, and I were so close. Sorry, Sarah: you were just that bit younger and we used to leave you behind all the time.

We were in the same sporting clubs, so we were all very close and are still very involved in each other's lives. I don't remember spending that much time with my dad's side of the family as mum and dad were divorced when I was younger. I probably see more of dad's side of the family now I'm older.

I'm quite close to Dad's sisters, my aunties, who are awesome fun – and Aunty Pat and Uncle John I see a lot of because they still live in Swan Hill. I do still see a lot of these cousins. Now that we are older, it's easier to get around. At family functions, we always have a great time. Dad, or Sambo as we call him, quite regularly checks in on me to make sure I'm okay.

Josh on Pee wee 50

Hayley mini four wheeler

Roberta, Steve, Darren, Gary, Bob, Brian & Pud Brian's family

Hayley at home

Jamie (brother) & Charlie

Katrina (sister) & Charlie

Paul (brother) & Charlie

Charlie & Sambo (dad)

Di (boss) & Charlie

Charlie, Maree, Jodi & baby Paige

Chapter 7:
Beginning My Work Life

"I learned English in a pub. I didn't learn it in school".
Guenther Steiner

My hospitality career started at the commercial hotel in Swan Hill. This is where I was taught to pour a beer and make mixed drinks. This pub could get extremely busy, with anywhere up to ten staff working behind the bar at the same time. It was a good place to learn how to deal with the pressure of having to serve several people all at once.

The hardest thing working here was that all my friends were on the other side of the bar, and all I wanted was to be drinking and partying with them. But unfortunately, I had no choice because I needed the money to pay rent and eat. This was probably my biggest reality check and welcome to the real world!

I lived with Maree and baby Paige first when I came home from Queensland. Aunty Lila lent me her old red Colt to get around in since I had written mine off. At least this way we had wheels to get around in, me, Maree, and baby Paigey. I then moved in with Jodi and Deanne. Maree should have just moved in with us because she practically lived there anyway, which was totally fine because we all wanted to help raise Paige.

The flat that we moved into was right next door to the original one where I had previously lived in with Kermie. He still lived there with

Fierce and Unstoppable

Shane, Pussa & Briany

our other cousin, Carolyn. She moved in when I moved out. These flats were called the Brown flats. They were upstairs with huge balconies and soon became the party houses. We used to call it Melrose Place because that's what it was like: people always coming and going day, and night.

Those were the days: we had a lot of great times. We used to make our own sambuca and then drink it out of 2-litre cordial bottles. It was disgusting, but it was cheap to drink, so we used to charge up on that before we went out. At some stage, the girls gave me a birthday gift. He was called Party Pete. He was a 6-foot blow-up penis. It was hilarious, so he took pride and place in our lounge room. We used to sit on him, hug him, and use him as a punching bag. The day he went flat was a sad funeral.

At the back of Kermie's flat, there was this old shed. We got home from the pub one night and thought it would be a good idea to do a séance. Something weird happened that night: either a spirit came

Beginning My Work Life

Charlie & Michael on 21st bday

through – or something else – and it frightened the shit out of all of us. We never did that again.

It wasn't long after moving in I put in a resumé at the Federal Hotel. I got a call for an interview. I was so excited because I had been looking for permanent work since I got home from Queensland. The interview involved sitting around on chairs with Joe and Di, who were soon to become my new employers. They offered me the job then and there; they also informed me that they had firstly handed my resumé around the bar for the patrons to have a look at. Philip Chisholm, who was a regular, read my resumé and said, "Hire this girl straight away." So I thank you, Chissy, because if it weren't for you, my life wouldn't have taken the course that it did.

I started my traineeship straight away, doing split shifts: one in the morning; one in the afternoon into the evening. I loved working

Julie Charleson

here straight away. The people were awesome, and my bosses were cool.

At first, after I finished my shift on a Saturday night, the girls would come to me, and we would still head over to the Commercial when I finished because that's where all the action was. This did change soon as word got around that there was a new bar maid at the Fed. It was quite funny because, suddenly, a lot of new faces started showing up to the pub.

My first encounter with the Hovenden boys was the night of my birthday. I was working; the girls had come over to visit with a birthday cake. When the girls came over, Maree always had with Paigey with her. She would just sit in the pram, and I would fill her bottle with raspberry soft drink.

Beginning My Work Life

Brian's business card

The girls were just having a drink when all the four brothers walked in. They had been at some rendering course and when it finished, they thought they would come for a beer. This was the first time I had met Brian and his brothers Stephen, Darren, and Bob. So, I served them and then they all started talking and started eating my cake – nothing like making themselves comfortable! So, as the night went on, we were all laughing. Everyone was having a good time, so I asked Steve if he would like a head job. He automatically dropped his pants, and we all burst out laughing because we knew what I'd actually meant – it was the name of a shot.

After that night, Brian suddenly started coming over to the pub each night, dragging poor old Bob with him, who lived with him at the time. One night, Brian ordered a drink and then handed over his money to pay for it. As I went to put the money in the till, I realised there was a business card with it. He had written "Harley Charlie" with his number on the card. He figured because the card didn't come back in the change that he was in for a chance. I kept it beside the till and took it with me when I finished work. I still have it in my drawer, and I'm so glad that I kept it for all these years.

He told Kylie, Bob's girlfriend, now sister-in-law, that, "I'm going to get that girl." Kylie just laughed and said, "I went to school with her. You don't stand a chance." We still laugh about the fact that I proved her wrong.

The next Saturday that I was working, Brian turned up on his Harley to take me for a ride during my break. He took me out to his friend's place, which was hilarious because as I took my helmet off, I knew Monica, poor Briany couldn't believe it. Anyway, we stayed there for the afternoon drinking until I had to go back to work. Brian stayed at the pub while I worked until knock off time, and then we went home together. That was the beginning of our love story.

Brian, at first, lied about his age to me. He tried to tell me he was only 28. I didn't believe him, but I just let him go. I think he felt he had to lie because he was so much older than me. It was funny he got caught out because my brother worked with a bloke that knew him. He said to him, "My sisters just started going out with Brian Hovenden, and he is 28." Millsy started laughing and said, "Bullshit. He's older than that; he's more like 35." Jamie couldn't believe it and came and told me straight away. I just laughed. I didn't care how old he was. The age thing was never a factor for me because he certainly never acted his age!

Telling Mum I was going out with a guy that was 35 and I was only 20, well, that was a different thing – until she met him, and then she loved him, so it didn't matter. All my friends at the time had the same opinion when they found out how old he was, but once they met him, they loved him too. He just had this charismatic personality that you couldn't help but love. He thought it was great. He always said, "You're only as old as the woman you feel," so he was feeling proud of himself.

I was still living at the flat at this time. I remember one time he was leaving early in the morning. At this stage, not everybody knew that we were going out, so he was trying to sneak out without anyone seeing him. As he got downstairs, he saw someone that he knew, so he ducked into the laundromat, took his jeans off and pretended that he was doing his washing. I laughed so hard when he told me this because I thought, *Did you really believe that bloke thought that's what you were doing?!*

We started spending all our time together. If I was at work, he was there after he finished as well. In those days, the Fed was a working man's pub, so all the tradies and workers from Pickering Transport, which was just across the road from the pub, came there for the five-dollar lunches, which were very popular.

Of a weekend, all the boys would all come for a counter lunch. I had to work split shifts during the week and weekends, which meant I had to work most nights. I didn't mind my hours because I loved working there. The patrons were fantastic. I have met so many people from there that have become lifelong best friends that I can rely on for any situation.

I could never call in sick to work because I was always drinking with my boss Joe the night before. One morning I came down the stairs of my flat, vomited into the pot plant, went to work, then lay on the floor in the bar. I also put my head in the fridge to try and sober up. Joe stitched me up again. We were drinking any drink you could think of!

I have so many stories to tell, but my favourite one is when I was driving past the Australian Settlers motel, which was owned by John and Julie Charleson. As I was driving past, they were both standing out the front. I was waving away and smiling at John because he was a regular over at the pub and I had come to know him quite well.

Apparently, he had been going home from the pub and talking about "Charlie this; Charlie that; the new person over at the Fed." Julie turned

Julie Charleson

to John and said, "Who was that?" John replied, "Oh, that's Charlie, the new barmaid at the Fed." She said, "What? No wonder you have been wanting to go over to the pub all the time. You never said she was young, had blonde hair, and tits!"

"This Friday night, you're staying home with the kids and I'm going to the pub and I'm going to check her out for myself." Well, she turned up Friday night and introduced herself. We had an instant connection and became great friends straight away. I then went on to spend a lot of time with Julie and her family, sitting around the pool at the motel with all our friends. Well, they couldn't leave, so we came to them.

Julie was one of my best friends. We spent all our time together. We left John at the motel this day and walked to the Monkey Bar, not far from the motel, parked ourselves at the bar, and got comfortable. A fight broke out by a guy I went to school with. It would have been fine if the barmaid had of just given him another drink; instead, stools went flying, police were called, and he got locked up. Anyway, we had cheap entertainment for the afternoon, so we thought we better head home. Julie was a party animal. We had a party at home one night instead of her going home with John-boy. We sent the kids home with him and she stayed with me.

This was a regular occurrence until this one day. I got the worst phone call in the world: Julie had passed away from an aneurysm. It broke my heart. I didn't want to believe it. I couldn't. I think about her all the time. It's been 20 years now. At least I still have great memories of her and thank God memories are the one thing that can never be taken away from you.

Another night when I was working, all the Hovo boys were there, and Brian was on crutches because he'd broke his leg at work. Anyway, the boys had a reputation for liking a fight, and they were pretty handy. This night a bloke was being a smart-arse to Steve, so Brian hopped over on his crutches and, while balancing on one crutch, smacked this bloke in the mouth.

Why the hell he thought he needed to protect Steve, I have no idea. I guess he just thought he was going to be the big brother and protect his younger one, which was a laugh, because we all know that Steve can handle himself better than probably any of them. Di, the owner, snuck this bloke out the back of the pub and drove him home before a bloodbath started.

I was smoking when I worked at the Fed. I used to smoke a pack of 30 PJ Super Milds a day. At that time, you were allowed to smoke behind the bar, so I had a smoke lit and then I would sit that down and go and pour a beer.

I was once whistled at behind the bar from a bloke who wanted a drink. Charlie Devil came out instantly, turned around and said, "I am not a fucking dog. Ask for a drink nicely, otherwise, turn around, walk out the fucking door and leave." Surprisingly, he apologised and then asked for a drink very, very politely. As I have said before, I didn't tolerate any bullshit, and I was not about to start now just because I was serving the public.

Working behind the bar, you meet many different personalities; you watch them come in sober and then watch them change as they drink. Some get angry, some cry, some laugh, some become very funny, while others just become extremely rude and obnoxious. It's amazing how alcohol can change people so much, especially when you are sober and get to sit back and watch with front-row seats.

My shift at work was from 10 until 2, then go back at 6 till 9 or close, depending on how busy it was. One of my favourite customers, first thing in the morning, was Darren Vearing. He would crawl out of the truck and come straight to the pub. I also became very good friends with his wife Chris, who is still one of my closest friends today.

I did split shifts for years, which I got used to. I had to serve the customers, take meal orders, bring meals out, sometimes work in the kitchen doing dishes, help cook, unpack the alcohol when it was delivered; this meant unpacking slabs and slabs of beer by hand. I was actually pretty fit by the end of it. Also, when I was behind the bar when a barrel ran out, I had to open the trap door in the floor, go down the stairs and change the barrels. I loved doing this. It was great. Then, because the pub was pretty old, I'd have to go back up and shake the shit out of the temprite and make it kick in so that the beer was cold.

It was a great job because I'm very social. I enjoyed it immensely, getting paid to talk to people all day. I knew all my customers very well.

Back then, you could leave your money on the bar. When I was serving them, I knew whose change was who's because of which drinks they were drinking.

The pub also had a TAB and pokies. Some days it was a lot to manage if I was working by myself, but Joe was never too far away as they lived on-site with their four children. I really couldn't have asked for better employers. They were more like family to me.

Having this job shaped my life. I met the love of my life and the most loyal people and best friends I could ever ask for to have in my life.

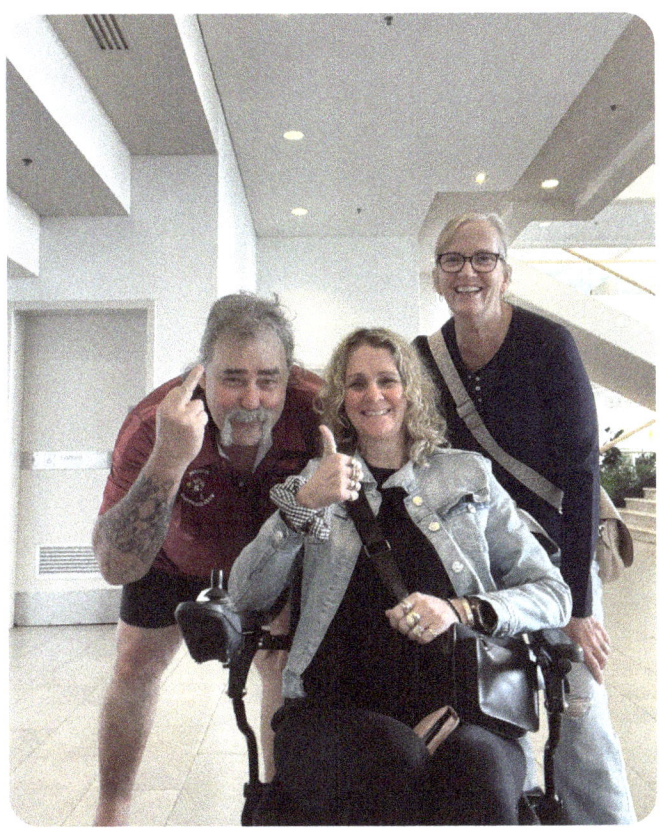

Vearo, Charlie & Christine

Brian & Charlie

Charlie & Brian (Bob & Kylie's wedding)

Chapter 8:
Love At First Sight

"Being deeply loved by someone gives you strength, while loving someone deeply gives you courage"

Lao Tzu

Do you believe in love at first sight? The first time I saw Brian he had a mullet, was dressed in jeans, a black jumper, and desert boots. If he didn't have his boots on, he was wearing thongs. What was not to love? We had an instant connection, and I think I did know then and there this was going to be a forever thing. He had a cheeky smile with a quick wit and always had the right words to say.

We all used to have a bit of a laugh because the young blokes started coming into the pub thinking they were going to have a crack at the young barmaid, but the old boy swept in and took over. It was like an unwritten law: once I started going out with Brian, I was not to be touched by anyone else. When I first started working, there a couple of blokes gave me a really hard time behind the bar, but instead of apologising to me, they rode their bikes out to home and apologise to Brian, I was like, *What the fuck?!*

I worked at the Fed until Joe and Di decided to sell, so then I decided to leave too. I got work at a local café for a little while, but this didn't work out. Then Brian's dad, Pud, offered me a job at the Plaster Works to start doing all the bookwork.

Fierce and Unstoppable

Brian & Charlie wedding day eloping

As our relationship grew, we just became each other's lives. We became one. I met all his mates and he met mine. Brian had a wide variety of close friends as well. Noel was a big part of his life; Billy, Ernie, JD, Shane, Dill, Franko, Ant, Spana, Wig, Tim, Peter, Roger, Merv, Terry, and so many more that I can't even name – plus all their partners who I became very close with. We hadn't been living together long, and he was away when I got the phone call that Zeke, one of his oldest mates, had hung himself. This had to have been one of the hardest things I ever had to tell him. It broke him; I had never seen him like that before. It was terrible.

Brian and I moved in together. He had a place just out of town on a small farm with a few acres. When I moved in, he'd only just planted all the trees around the boundary and there was only a couple of taps, so we had to fill buckets up and water them all by hand.

There was no lawn. There was nothing. The house was very old, with the old verandah and a fly wire all around it. When Brian first brought me out here, I asked him, "Do you really live here?" He took

Love At First Sight

Josh, Charlie, Hayley & Brian

me to the front door and said, "I'll just unlock it." He did this by reaching his hand through the fly wire and just unlocked the door. I wasn't sure what to think at first, but I soon fell in love with the old shack.

The paddocks were on irrigation, so Brian had to water every few weeks. Because I had grown up on a farm, I suggested that we get some little calves, bucket feed them, fatten them up, and then sell them. We did this for quite a few years. I loved it: mixing up the milk and then pouring it in the feeders hanging on the gate for the calves to come and feed from. It was hard yakka, and I did it by myself for a fair while until I wasn't fit enough anymore to carry the buckets and lift them up over the gate. I just wasn't strong enough to do it after a while. So, then Brian took over.

There was a process with the cows. We had to feed them pellets next to fatten them up and then hay. We had to buy some temporary cattle yards, and my mum actually gave us a crush so we could run them in this, to hold them, needle them, and then take them to sale. Brian

Hayley, Charlie, Josh & Brian wedding certificate

was a bit of a sook: he wouldn't needle them. I had to pull the skin back and shove the needle in and inject them. We also had to drench them, which meant pouring the drench down their back. Brian could handle this. Finally, we had to ear tag them, fill out all the paperwork, and then put them in the trailer and take them to sale. We made quite good money out of them. It was a bit of work, but it was worth it. Our most busy time was when we had 20 head of cattle, which was a lot on our little farm.

We had been together for years when I fell pregnant with Josh, our first child. I was 23. Josh was born 23rd August 2001. My waters broke at home with Josh, but I had to ring my sister-in-law, Tracey, to pick me up because Brian wouldn't leave work. We were shocked as he was a little surprise that just popped along.

Brian wouldn't tell his parents that I was pregnant. I had to go and do it. I don't know why he was scared about that because his parents were over the moon. He always said he never wanted children, but when

Love At First Sight

Brian & Josh

they came along, bloody hell, he was the best father in the world. He just doted on them and loved them to pieces.

When Josh was about six months old, he kept getting bitten by spiders and insects. The old shack wasn't exactly insect-proof, so Brian decided we would build a new house. We knocked the old house down and put a relocatable behind bit in. This made it very easy to move because the houses were side-by-side on the front lawn.

Secondly, we had Hayley, when I was 26, on the 26th August 2004. We had tried for a year to have her. Brian didn't want to come near me in the end. He always said Hayley was his hardest work of all. When you're trying to get pregnant and you can't, it is the biggest rollercoaster of your life. Just waiting each month to see if that period would turn up or not. They were both August babies, having been conceived around my birthday. Brian always thought my birthday was a sure thing for him to get lucky – I had to remind him it was my

Original house (the shack)

birthday, not his – or Christmas parties. Drunken sex always brings out the best. Their birthdays are only three days apart. There is three years between them, which meant when Hayley was 18, Josh would be 21. Brian always thought this was great as they could have a joint party. My thoughts were, *Fantastic 18-year-old girls and 21-year-old boys – can you imagine the hormones floating around?!*

Well, after Hayley, it was work as usual. I went back to work two weeks after having Josh and three weeks after having Hayley, with both of them in toe with me. When I went into labour with Hayley, we were on our way to the hospital and I said to Brian, "We need to make a quick stop at work." He looked at me as if to say, *What the fuck?* I waddled inside to order a load of plaster, got that done, back in the car, and off to hospital. My contractions were two minutes apart. She was born a few hours later. Hey, at least I got the plaster ordered!

Love At First Sight

Charlie & Brian

My office was set up like a crèche. It had the cot, blackboard, and all the toys in the corner. Brian's dad, Pud, who they called Pop, was there to help me a lot. He used to push the kids around in the pram or the trolley. They just adored their pop and were lucky enough

Charlie, Brian, Hayley & Josh

to spend so much time with him. Pop smoked a pack of Benson & Hedges Special Filter a day. The kids always asked him why he smoked. His answer was always to keep his nose warm!

Our kids grew up in the business and around people all the time, so they were brought up to be very social, being handed around as babies to builders or whoever was there to hold them. We also never stopped our social life when the children came along. They got dragged around to all our friends' places and to parties, wherever we went, so did they.

After we had been together for years, had the kids and the house, we decided to get married. I wasn't too worried about the whole marriage thing – only that I wanted to have the same last name as my children, since I went all through most of my schooling life with a different surname to my mother, and it was very confusing at times.

I went and bought the ring myself and Brian put it on my finger one night in the kitchen – very romantic, I know. We were going to have

Love At First Sight

Charlie, Hayley, Brian & Josh

a wedding, started to make a list, and it all just became too hard, so we went off to the registry office and eloped. The only people we had with us were the kids and Bob and Kylie as our witnesses. Afterwards we took the kids to Luna Park; this was as close to a honeymoon as I ever got!

Three years later, it was my 30th. We had a thong party theme, whether you wore them on your feet or elsewhere. We combined it with our post-wedding party and had a surprise mock wedding. One of our friends was the priest. He dressed up as Elvis and made up vows to this theme. I walked out to the song, *I Was Made For Lovin' You* by Kiss. It was hilarious and so much fun. If I had my time again, I wouldn't do a thing different.

As the kids got older, we bought them motorbikes, which they rode around the paddock like crazy cats. Then they had old cars to drive around. This was a great experience for them and they loved it. They became involved in sport. Josh played footy, but not for very long as he wanted to play but not have to train; Hayley played netball and loved it. She still plays now – she developed her mother's competitive streak.

Next, Hayley did her Deb ball which another mother, Robyn Reed, and I organised. It was the first of the balls to be held outside at the Jockey club in February, so the weather was perfect. The night was amazing. Hayley's solo part involved her being completely flipped over to land back on her feet. I was so proud, and she looked absolutely stunning. She was lucky enough to have danced with her father because, at this time, we didn't know, but this would never happen again. This is why we must treasure all these times whenever we can.

Brian had sold his Harley years before. I never wanted him to, but it was his decision because he wanted to buy a fishing boat. The whole family could fit in that much easier than on the bike! Our next adventure was to buy our vintage cars, a '56 Chevrolet Wagon, a '57 Chevrolet Bel Air and then lastly, a '59 Chevrolet pick-up ute – all left-hand drive. These became his babies which he absolutely loved.

I haven't really touched base on what it was like to become a mother. Once you have children, they become your life. You love them with your whole body and soul. As soon as you hold them in your arms, your life instantly changes. All of a sudden, you have this little life in your hands that you have to care for, not knowing what to do or how to look after them properly.

Unfortunately, there is no book on how to be a perfect parent. Most of the time we're just winging it and hoping that we do a good job. We can only give advice and hope that they take it. Whether they do or not is a completely another matter. My two children are complete opposites. Josh is like his father, quite placid most of the time and tries to calm situations. Hayley? Well, she is a firecracker. Let's just say the apple didn't fall far from the tree of her mother. She used to tell me hate me several times a day when she was little. My reply was, "Good. That means I am doing my job right. I am here to be your mother not your best friend!"

I can honestly say I am proud of my children. They both made it through school with a few ups and downs. They've also worked hard. Josh started his apprenticeship as a plasterer at 15. When I rang the school to say he was leaving, his teacher told me he was making the right decision, so I'm pretty sure they were happy to get rid of him. Hayley finished year 12, and she, too, started her apprenticeship as a plasterer, but didn't finish hers, mainly because Brian died.

She then went on to get her Certificate III in Individual Support (Disability), which she is still working at now. She also works at Worklocker, the Jockey Club, the plaster works, does waitressing, and caring for myself. On the weekends during winter, she plays netball, and in the summer, she spends a lot of time out the lake. At the age of 20 now she is living her best life, going out, meeting people, and having fun, which is exactly what I want her to do.

They now have both bought their own homes, which I know their father would be very proud of. Josh is a father now, at 23, with a beautiful little girl, Billie, which makes me a grandmother, which I am still coming to terms with… At the end of the day, if circumstances occurred, I would trade my life for both of theirs quite happily as I'm sure any parent would. Well, at least 90% of the time anyway. Sometimes children do annoy us… Only joking! I definitely would at any time.

I just have to tell this story of when Hayley was young and being a right little so-and-so. I yelled at her, so she started running down the back lawn. There was a box of lemons on the table. I picked one up

– bearing in mind, I can't throw for shit – and I threw it at her as hard as I could. Bugger me! Dead bullseye! I got her right in the back of the head, and it dropped her to the ground.

We all burst out laughing as her little pink Crocs went flying. She would have only been about five. I am still laughing as I write this because even Hayley said that story will never get old. I love them around the world and back. I hope they both know this. I do make a point of telling them I love then almost every day, as we never know which one will be our last.

Now, my relationship with Brian, it was a one-and-only. If you're lucky in life to have loved, and I mean really loved, consider it a privilege because not everybody gets that chance. This kind of love is a rare commodity that we take for granted. Like I said, not many people can say they have loved and been loved unconditionally. I think I am one of the lucky few to have been lucky enough to have met my one and only.

We very rarely had a fight or a bad argument, and even if we did. Brian couldn't stand it. He would come in and do something stupid and make me laugh so I would talk to him again. We were never one of these couples that went days or weeks without speaking if there was a disagreement. We just didn't really have any need to. We were kindred spirits that were just meant to be together.

We worked together all day, went home together, had a drink together, tea, and then bed. He would ring me at 8 o'clock every morning just to check in and make sure that I was okay. When he got his new iPhone, he learnt to FaceTime, so then he would ring each morning. If I'd been up early and was ready and dressed, he was pissed off that he missed me with no clothes on or just in my underwear and couldn't see me on his phone. Sometimes he would come home just to try and catch me in the shower!

I know my children aren't going to want to read this, but our love life was very active and he was 60! So for all you ladies who are hoping it wears off as they get older, I am here to burst your bubble – it gets worse. An older lady once told me, "You keep their belly full and their balls empty and they will never leave you!" I'm hoping people are laughing at this statement because they know it's true… We all know a man's brain is not in his head; it's between their legs.

Brian had to be constantly touching me, which was nice, but sometimes, it was just fucking annoying. It became a game to him – to touch my arse and see if he could do it without anyone seeing him. He got caught all the time but thought he didn't, which was even funnier. If he wasn't around me all the time he would fret. If he drove somewhere, he would ring me and talk to me the whole way!

It's nice to think that someone loves you that much that they never want to be away from you. Like I said, love like that doesn't come around every day. I just count myself lucky that he came into my life and he was mine. He was my soulmate, best friend, and the love of my life, which I think only comes around once in a lifetime – if you are lucky xx

This song sums us up as a couple – ***Two of us - Louie Tomlinson***

Charlie & Hayley

Love At First Sight

Hayley & Brian

Original plaster shed

Hovenden's Plaster Works 2022

Chapter 9:
Becoming Business Owners

"There has to be a balance in life. A balance of business, family, and the opportunity to learn and teach"

Chuck Feeney

Brian had only ever worked for his father for most of his life until we took over the business. He wanted to be a motor mechanic until his dad said to him one day, "Just come and try this," and he never left. His father owned a plastering business, and he was a plasterer himself. He had a team of men that worked for him. Brian soon joined in 1977, which made him 15.

Funnily enough, he started the year I was born. Brian's dad started his career in Kerang and then moved to Swan Hill to start his own business. He had his own team of men that worked for him. They were all older and used to give Brian a smack under the ear when he started, especially when he fell asleep in the ceiling one day.

This trade became Brian's passion, and as the years went on, he trained all three of his three younger brothers, who all worked for their father also. The business started off in a small shed in his back yard until he expanded it, and then when we bought it, we expanded it more. They were big in contracting, commercial, and residential. They travelled far and wide in The Mallee. They were the main contractors in town, worked for the majority of the local builders, as well as ones in Hopetoun and Balranald.

Hayley in plaster shed

There weren't many houses in Swan Hill that the boys hadn't plastered, and the Hovendens were very well-known – they still are. Every house they worked in they would write their name in the ceiling. Every time someone finds his name, I get a photo of it. One builder, Dobbo, cut out a whole beam and brought it into me. I was so grateful have that piece of him.

Their work utes were Dyna Toyota dual cabs with trestles on the racks and a tub in the back to fill all their tools in. They weren't the most comfortable vehicle – no air-conditioning – but the boys just got in, did the job, and did what had to be done. They had t stilts, which they wore on their legs, so they could reach higher to the ceilings without needing scaffolding all of the time. It always amazed me how they walked around on their stilts so easily, jumped up onto them, strapped them on, and off they went.

Dyna work Utes

Brian's dads name was Brian too but he was just known as Pud. Plaster or gypsum must have run in the Hovendens' veins because Pud ended up with four sons, four grandsons, and a granddaughter, who all ended up in the trade. Then there was me, his daughter-in-law. It truly was a family business.

I worked side-by-side with Pud for many years. He taught me how to quote, about all the plaster products, the running of the business, and how to handle the builders. Pud was a great teacher. He was so patient. Then it became a competition between us every time: we quoted and we had to compare our prices to decide whose price was correct. We would both argue our reasons and debate against each other until we made a decision.

We also got caught out many times as customers would ring wanting to know why the boys weren't at their job. I would lie and blame Pud; he would lie and blame me until they came into the shed and we were sitting together. Well, then, we had to think fast and come up with a bullshit story.

Fierce and Unstoppable

Bob, Drew, Josh. Brian on scissor lift

I started working for Hovendens Plaster Works in the year 2000. I wasn't entirely sure how it would go working with Brian and his family, but it was fine. I loved working there. Pud became like a father to me and I loved him dearly. He actually helped raise Josh and Hayley as they grew up in the plaster shed. They had been there since they were babies. It got to a time when Pud was ready to retire. There were only two sons left working in the business by now, Bob and Brian.

Bob didn't want to buy into the business. Instead, he went out on his own contracting, so Brian and I bought the business in 2011. This was a huge scary step, but it was now or never, so we took the leap, went to the bank, and bought the business off Brian's parents and never looked back. We grew the business. It was Brian's dream, and it had finally come true. We stayed in the contracting and had a staff of 10 at one stage, which took some looking after.

Becoming Business Owners

Hovenden's Plaster Works workers

Briany, as he was known by everyone, looked after all the blokes and I did all the quoting, books, and dealt with a lot of the builders as Brian didn't like the confrontation, even though he was a better bullshit artist than me. I would like to think we were a power couple working together. A lot of people didn't know how we did it, working together and living together. I tell you how: because we were a team and just liked being around each other 24/7. Occasionally, I did need a break and told him to go for a drive, but he would just go to the servo, get me a chocolate bar, and come back.

We stayed in the contracting for years until we decided to cut back on that side of things and go into the supply side of the business. Briany loved his trade and was a wealth of knowledge about it. He lived and breathed plaster. We had always supplied plaster and compounds, but Briany wanted to go bigger, so we extended the shed to be

Josh plastering

able to cater and he made it work: the shed was filled with plaster, insulation, and compounds. His idea worked, and we still now run a very successful business.

Don't get me wrong, business is hard work and takes a lot of time, stress, and commitment. But this would not be possible without great suppliers: Uosif at Bell Plaster; Frankie at Madex Plaster; Bevo at Fletcher Insulation; also, our freight company Pickering Transport. Last but not least, none of it would be possible without our amazing loyal customers. I don't look on them as customers but as family. I can rely on them for anything. There are too many to name, but I will put in a photo of our Christmas party just to give you a bit of an idea of the support they give myself and my kids.

I think Briany's proudest moment was when Josh decided to become a plasterer and started and finished his apprenticeship. Then again,

Becoming Business Owners

Owen, Brian & DD

when Hayley decided to do her apprenticeship, she didn't finish hers. I think after Brian passed it was just too hard for her. She is still a part of the business, occasionally going out to help Josh on the tools, otherwise she helps to run the shed. I'm surprised sometimes at the knowledge the children have about the business after all these years. I thought they weren't paying attention; instead, they were like little sponges.

There are so many funny stories about Brian's working life. He had to try and keep all the builders happy, so his theory was just "put someone on every job". This one day we were working for one of his good friends, who was a builder – they both started in the building trade at the same time – and they had a nickname for each other: "two dicks". Don't ask me how this came about because I'm not sure. But this day Brian was supposed to be working on his job, instead Brian went and parked his Ute at the work site and put all the doors of it up. So that when the builder turned up to the job, he thought Briany was there. He went inside expecting to see Brian, but he only saw the electrician. He asked him if he had seen Brian. He said, "No one's been here." Little did Snail know, as soon as Brian got there and set up his Ute, he rang Hayley to come and pick him up. We all still laugh about that day.

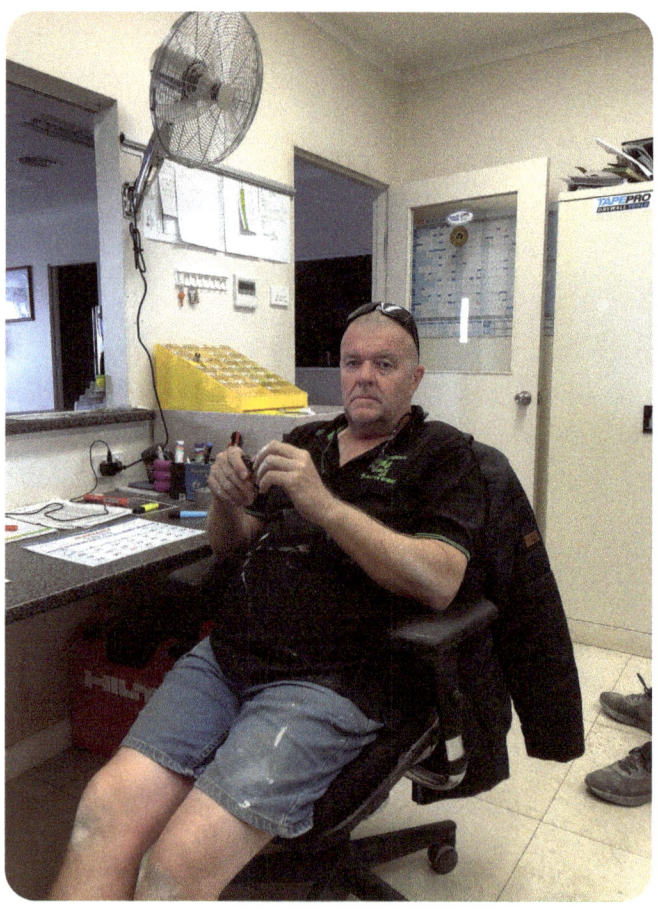

Brian at work

Brian loved working. He would go in sometimes at three or four in the morning or work on Sundays, which never bothered me. I didn't care. He was happy. He loved his great big white shed. Even when we were home during holidays, he had to go to his shed every day just to get a fix. I could keep talking about him, but anyone who knew him knows how good of a man he was – and that he was an absolute gossip! All the tradies came there to find out what was going on because what he didn't know wasn't worth knowing. All his workers and the customers loved him, and they all have their own stories as he was a very funny man and a practical joker.

Because I worked with tradesmen mainly, I had a reputation of telling them exactly how it was: I swear and carry on and do as I please. If I didn't swear at some of my customers, they would wonder what was wrong with me. I can be good: I know who to swear in front of and who not to.

I have also been known on occasion to swear at my suppliers (I can hear Frankie and Justin laughing right now), especially Pickering if they don't deliver my shit on time or if it's damaged.

But I don't apologise for my behaviour because when you're working in the trade, full of men, you have to adapt and just become one of them. Besides, I've been working on my reputation for over 20 years. I'm not about to change now. I will not stand around and let anyone walk over me easily. Some think they can because I am a woman, but they are in for a shock. My tongue is like giving you whip lash sometimes.

Also I have to say, running a business is not easy. At times, it can be very stressful, especially when there is not enough money in the account to pay the bills. It becomes a juggling act. But I had a good relationship with my bank manager. I never told Brian about this; he just would have panicked.

This business would never have been able to run without my professionals on-call all the time. Chloe, my bank manager, Brad, my accountant, trusted friend and counsel – I have broken down and cried on him more times than I can count. I try not to do this to many people; I would be lost without him.

He is a great friend. Then there is my lawyer who is on a retainer that I have never paid for over 15 years. We always have a joke about my pretend bins in my office they are called the C U Next Tuesday bins and whoever has pissed me off that ends up in one. I can tell you some days they are full!

Again, these people are all my great friends who I can call on at any time. I have to make a special mention to my number one employee, Eli Keating, I am his work mum, and he is very valuable to us.

Our 2023 work Christmas Party

Becoming Business Owners

Hayley & Brian

Steve, Josh, Bob & Brian (Josh with uncles & dad)

Fierce and Unstoppable

Pickerings transport truck sign writing

Becoming Business Owners

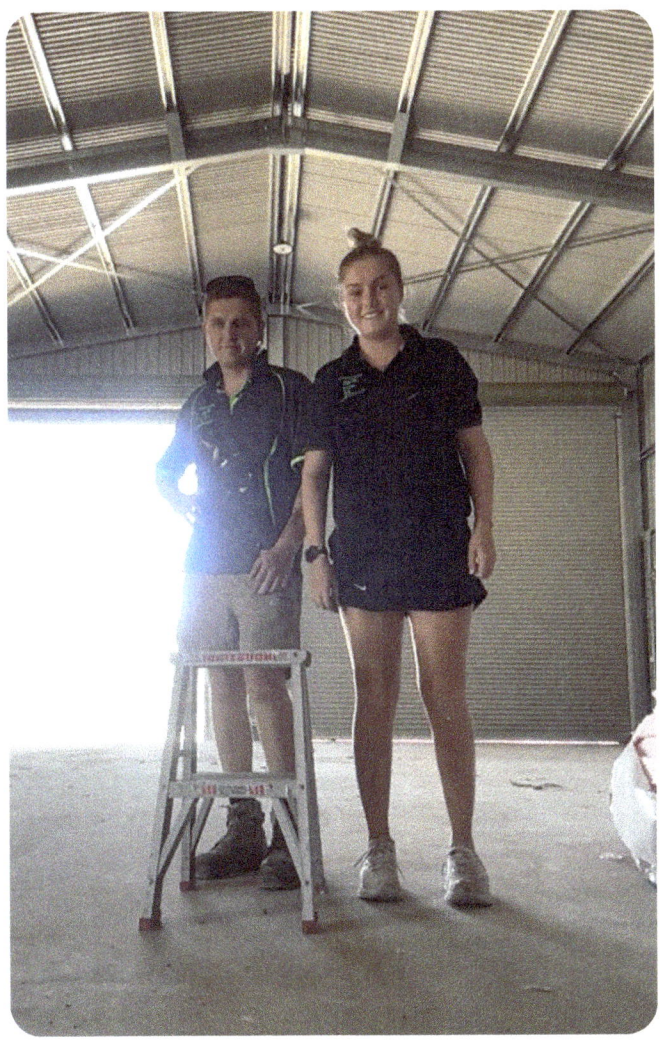

Hayley & Josh 2025

Part 2:
My Journey With MS

From:

Sent: Thursday, 26 October 2006 12:35 AM

Subject: Charlie

Hey guys,

I'm writing to all my oldest and dearest friends to let them all know that over the past month or so, I have been back and forth to doctors, neurologists and have been diagnosed with MS, so all those years we all thought my knees were fucked, it was really the MS doing the damage. Hey, at least now I have an excuse to walk like a retard. So, from the 8th Nov, I have to start injecting a drug on a weekly basis to try and stop the progression of the disease from getting worse.

The disability in my leg will never get any better so you will all have to just get used to the gimpy walk, ha ha ... Although it won't get any better, hopefully the injection will stop it from getting any worse or slow it down at least. Who knows I may end up in a wheelchair years to come but I will deal with that when it happens.

I could quite easily do with a walking stick at the moment, I always had the pram to hold on to and that acted as my walking frame, but my little girl is growing up and really doesn't want to be in that all that much anymore.

Please don't be sad, I'm not. I had a fair bit of time to deal with it, and it sure as hell explains a lot to me, but I will most likely need a bit of support over the next few months, and I want strong happy friends to help me get through this and we all have to learn to cope with it. I must admit, I was hoping he would pump me full of steroids so I could walk normal, but hey at least I'm still alive, and it's not a fatal disease, just sometimes a disabling one.

So, I stress to you that I'm not going to die any time soon and will still be able to laugh and swear and carry on like we always have. I'm allowed to have a few drinks, nothing excessive but I will judge that as I go. I don't whether many of you know much about the disease, but there are so many websites to get onto and read about it and being aware of things makes things a lot easier.

Ok so I guess I'll wait to hear from you, and I am fine, but I don't want any tears from you or that will make me start too, so just happy faces ok.

Love you all.
Charlie

Hayley's message to mum

Chapter 10:
My Diagnosis

"If you can't find the sunshine, be the sunshine"

Fatima Karim

Firstly, I want to make one thing very clear as you read this: I don't want pity or you to feel sorry for me. I just want understanding. A few sniffles and tears are okay, I suppose, and I occasionally I need a hug, but you need to save your watery eyes for the next part. Don't waste them all just yet because I am strong and will push my body to its absolute limits to cope. You all know this already.

I started noticing things were different with my body. My balance, coordination, and walking were all up to shit. I was still trying to play netball, but I couldn't catch the ball. It went straight through my hands. When I tried to shoot a goal, I didn't even have this strength to push the ball up. The last thing that tipped me over before I went and saw the doctor was, as I tried to walk up the steps at home, I fell and tripped. Brian said, "Well, what did you do that for?" I turned around and replied, "Well, if I fucking knew, I wouldn't have done it would I?!"

I knew then that something was wrong, so I went and saw my GP, Stewart Booth, who had been my doctor for years and years. He referred me to an orthopaedic surgeon because he thought that it was my ankle. When I got to see my ortho, I remember this like it was yesterday. I lay down on the table and he checked my ankle, but then he did another test – which I wasn't expecting – on my toes. With my eyes closed, he bent my toes up and down, especially my big toes, and I couldn't tell him whether he was bending them up or down. I couldn't feel them. After I did this, he said, "Well, I could fix your ankle –" I had had an ankle reconstruction years before "– but I'm pretty sure that's not the problem. I need to refer you to a colleague of mine. He is a neurologist." I started to panic a little bit because I thought a neurologist was just to do with your brain.

Next thing I knew, I was in the office of Professor Chris Bladin who worked out of a private practice in Box Hill. I was very nervous, and so was Brian. He took me to all my appointments and was there by my side for everything. Professor Bladin did a series of tests as well. The scariest one is the balance test. I know it sounds silly, but you need to try it for yourself. I had to stand and try to balance with my eyes closed. I didn't want to do it because I felt like I was going to fall over.

He kept telling me to close my eyes and balance, I kept telling him, "No, I don't want to do it." He said, "It's okay; I will catch you if you fall." Against my instincts, I had to do it and trust him. Thankfully, I didn't fall. Once all the testing was finished, we went and sat down in his office. I knew it wouldn't be good news because I had read the referral from the orthopaedic that he had sent, and in the letter, it said I had hyperreflexia. So, what do you do? Google, of course.

I Googled what it meant and the first thing that came up in the search was "motor neurones". I couldn't control it. Tears just started flowing down my cheeks. I was thinking the absolute worst, so when I got to the neurologist and I was sitting in the chair, he told me he was "99% sure" that I had multiple sclerosis. I know this will sound stupid, but I actually felt a little bit of relief because I knew this disease may disable me, but, hopefully, not kill me – not quickly anyway.

I cried in the office when he gave me the news. Brian stood there in shock. I don't think he completely knew the extent of multiple sclerosis. I dried my tears, put my big-girl pants on, and asked the doctor, "Okay, so what do I do now? What are my options? What do I do next?" He went on to explain. "I want you to go home and read as much as you possibly can about this disease. The more you know, the better you will be to handle it. We also need to do an MRI just to confirm the diagnosis, but I know this will be the outcome."

He went on to explain the first treatment that I would be starting on, which he hoped would be a good start for me. At least now having a diagnosis explained a lot of things. I started to think back, and I think this disease had been coming for a long time. There were so many signs that I just didn't pick up on. Well, I wasn't expecting that news. I was always hoping it was going to be something simple, something that would be easy to fix, not a disease with no cure.

Brian actually gave me a hug when we got out of the doctor's office, which was unusual for him to do in public. I figured I had to play the strong one because I wasn't sure how he was going to cope either. This now would impact our lives forever.

We got into the car, and I said, "Well, on a positive note, I can at least start using a walking stick now. That might stop me from falling over as much and I have an excuse to use one." I was pretty happy about this. Now, to go home and tell all the friends and family about my diagnosis. Telling my mum was going to be the hardest because I knew she would cry, and nobody likes to see their mother cry.

I had already made up my mind that I needed to stay strong for my children, husband, friends, and the rest of my family. I could have rolled up into a ball and just let myself lie there and feel sorry for myself, but that wasn't my personality. I thought, *Fuck this. I'm not letting my disease beat me*. So with determination and resilience, I decided the show must go on. It was easier that my children were only young because they then just grew up with mum on a walking stick and they never knew any different for a long time.

Having Hayley in the pram was a blessing because it was like a walking frame, I was pissed off when she started to walk and wouldn't go in the pram anymore. Of course, she was little-miss-independence and walked at 9 months. If I buckled her in, she amazingly undid it and climbed out! Could she not have been like her brother and only started walking when she was 14 months old? It would have given me a little more time.

Once everyone found out, a lot of friends came to me and apologised because we had always made fun of the way I walked. I never cared about those things. If you don't laugh, you cry. Maree always told me that I walked like a newborn calf. I found this very funny because it was true. I had the support and love of everyone, so I was lucky. Not once did the love of my husband waver throughout the whole time. He ran me everywhere, to appointments in Melbourne constantly, and not once ever complained. He could've walked away. I know plenty of others that have, but there was no way he was doing that. His whole mindset changed. Everything became about my health.

I was diagnosed in 2006 when I was 29 years old, but the neurologist said I had possibly had it for 7 to 10 years before that and looking back now, I can see that it was absolutely true. All these years, I thought it was just my knees and my ankles, because I had a knee reconstruction at 16, then an ankle reconstruction a couple of years later. Then, when Josh was 6 months old, I had to have a knee patella stabilisation because my kneecap was wearing out. I had to retire from playing netball at 19. I thought it was strange, but my coordination just wasn't there anymore. That was the main thing that I was most pissed off about because I loved my netball. Everything else I was happy to give up.

Hayley was two years old and Josh was five. This was the saddest part because I knew I would never be able to run around with them, throw a ball, or even be able to pick them up again without falling over. But believe me, as they got older, they used this to their advantage. They knew I couldn't chase them, so when they were in trouble, they used to run around the couch from side to side – little shits – because they knew I couldn't catch them. There was one thing they didn't count on though: my walking stick had a pretty good reach and got wrapped around their bums quite frequently.

I continued to work. This was what kept me going: having to get up and actually do something every day. Plus, I love our customers. I love talking to them. That was my specialty and still is. I love to talk. Just go back and ask all my teachers in school. That was what I always got in trouble for – talking too much in class! Just ask Peppy, even though he knew everything I'd done on the weekend by the time I got to class on Monday!

The majority of our customers that come in wouldn't even have known that I had MS as I was always sitting in a chair. I never said anything, and if they asked me what was wrong, I just replied, "Oh, it's just a permanent thing." I never went into detail unless they genuinely seemed interested.

After another couple of visits with Professor Bladin and he referred me to the MS clinic at Box Hill to my new neurologist, Professor Helmut Butzkueven. He was German, if you hadn't already guessed that by his name. I have been seeing him every year for 20 years, so he knows me pretty well by now. He knows that I swear and carry on and the rules are that he's always to tell me the truth and no bullshit, which, to his credit, he has always done.

I trust him with all my heart that he will do everything that he can possibly do to help me. I can contact him at any time on his mobile, which is fantastic, except sometimes he is overseas as he does a lot of travel to try and discover any new research that can help this disease. He is very clever and truly knowledgeable, so everything I ask, I trust to be the right answer.

I don't very often complain about my disease. There is no point. Just deal with it and move on: strength and positive thinking in yourself is the only true thing you can count on. Power of the mind is a very powerful to have. This is the course of my life and we cannot change things that have already happened. *So toughen the fuck up, princess, buckle up, and hold on for the ride.*

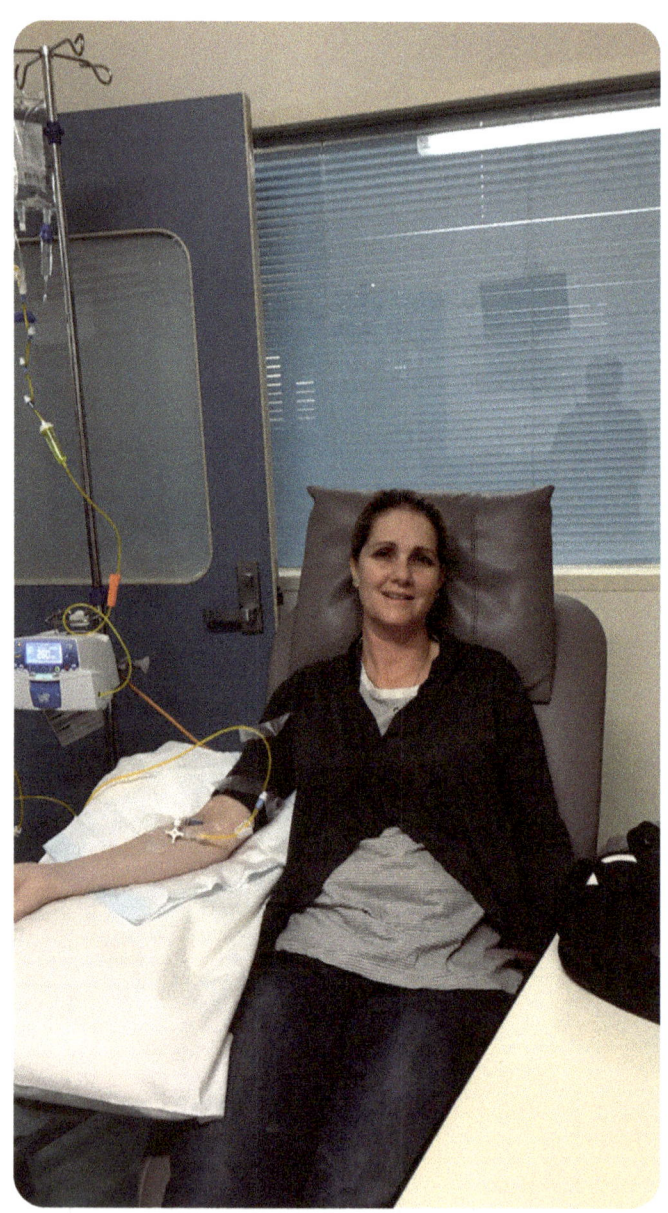
Charlie having treatment

Chapter 11:
Medication

"The strongest people are not those who show strength in front of the world but those who fight and win battles that others do not know anything about."

Jonathan Harnisch

Being in my first stage of MS was called relapsing remitting, which meant you would go along fine, have a relapse, have some steroids, then, hopefully, bounce back to where you were before, which I did for many years. A relapse is when your body becomes extremely tired and just can't function the way it was at the time. This is why I was given steroids, to try and stop the inflammation on the spinal cord, which is causing the relapse.

MS can be a disabling disease; this happens because around your spinal cord is an insulation which is called the myelin sheath. The disease develops lesions on the spine which then attack the myelin sheath and destroy it on your spine, which, in turn, affects walking, balance, and all those wonderful things that help keep you on your feet. You can also get lesions on your brain. My biggest lesion is on my brain stem, which stops messages from getting to my legs, and that's what makes me trip and fall all the time. So here my journey begins, and what a rollercoaster it is, trying every drug they threw my way. I was always up for the challenge to try anything.

My first medication I started was called AVONEX. This involved injecting myself once a week. It wasn't an EpiPen but an actual needle that had to be put into the skin and then pushed for the drug to get in. I had my own nurse assigned to me that came up from Melbourne to teach me how to needle myself properly. I was given a sponge to practise on. I had to learn to drop my hand and just let it fall into the sponge. The needle was extremely sharp, so it pierced the skin very easily.

My first time, I was very nervous. I had never had to do anything like this before. I went along fine for a few months until, suddenly, the nerves got me and I couldn't do it. So I poured myself a bourbon to get up some extra courage to be able to do it. Brian couldn't watch. He used to have to go outside, kept standing at the door and asking, "Have you done it yet?" Nothing like getting a bit of extra pressure on me!

The kids were braver than Brian. They used to stand on the couch with their little heads, just peering over and watching. They would say, "Mummy, come on. You can do it," as they were only two and five. Finally, I got it in that night, but the next week, I took it to work just in case I had to go to the hospital and get them to do it. I went into the toilet at work to have a bit of privacy, but Pud was just as bad as Brian, standing outside the door, "Have you done it yet? Do you need a bourbon? I'll go and get you one."

Eventually, I stopped trying to drop my hand to put the needle in and realised the needle was so sharp, I could just sit it on my leg and push it in. The nurse had explained that you only have to just pierce the skin, get past that first little nerve, and then you don't feel anything. I stayed on the AVONEX, but it wasn't working because I kept relapsing every three months, which meant I had to have a 1000mg-a-day dose of methylprednisolone for three consecutive days. This drug had to be administered, again, by an infusion at the hospital, I became a pin cushion because my veins were so shit.

The drug was supposed to go in over four hours, but I was too impatient, and I made them push it in over an hour (I had to get back to work). It did hurt the veins a little bit. Hayley sometimes came and sat with me before she went to school. This drug worked, but the side-effects included insomnia and heart palpitations. It felt like your heart was jumping out of your chest. Then a few days later, your body becomes extremely sore to touch. Brian liked it when I couldn't sleep because it meant he got a tap on the shoulder and woken up in the middle of the night. Well, honestly, what else was I supposed to do? I had to pass the time somehow – everyone was a winner!

The next drug on the list was Tysabri, which was given through an infusion at the hospital once a month over four hours. I had to go to Melbourne for the first six doses because of possible side-effects, then the nurses in Swan Hill had to be trained how to dispense it. As I needed someone to take me, Sue Pickering took me each month, sat and waited with me, and then took me home afterwards for years. What a great friend to be able to do this for me. I loved her company and we spoke about many different topics as we had plenty of time to spare. She became a big part of my appointments and life.

Unfortunately, this drug didn't work either as I kept relapsing. Plus, I tested positive to possibly getting the brain disease, which was a side-effect. All of these drugs come with some sort of side-effect and, as usual, I was one of the lucky ones to test positive for risk of developing this one, so it had to be stopped instantly. Anyway, keep smiling and move onto the next one. I was glad because my veins couldn't take the infusions anymore. It would take the nurses at least three goes to try and find my vein.

The next drug was Gilenya. It was a tablet at once a day, which made me very happy. Though, once again, this drug didn't work either, so onto the next one. Helmut was trying everything he could to slow down the disease. The next drug was a little bit more intense: Lemtrada. I had to go into hospital in Melbourne for five days. This drug was to kill my whole immune system and try and restart it. I was also given 1000mg of methylpred a day for five days as well.

I was hooked up to an infusion for six hours a day while they pumped all these drugs into me. By the end of the five days, my body felt like it had been dragged through the ringer. On the last day, the neurologist came around to do his rounds, took one look at me and saw that I was completely exhausted, so he prescribed some sleeping tablets. I could finally get some rest. I had to have this drug for two years, but the second year was only for three days in hospital. Before I started this drug, I also had to be given other drugs to try and prevent side-effects. The biggest downfall of this drug was that I had to have a blood test once a month for five years. They needed to keep an eye on my blood to make sure that everything was okay, especially my thyroid, which went up and down like a yo-yo.

Once again, my trusty friend Sue drove me to Barham to have the blood test because I couldn't have it in Swan Hill. This went on for a couple of years until they finally realised that clinical labs could do the test. Unfortunately, once again, this drug still wasn't slowing the disease as much as we had liked. Another new drug had come out so Helmut decided to try me on that. This one was called MAVENCLAD I was very happy because this one was a tablet too. Then there was Mayzent and Ocrevus, which was another monthly infusion, and now, finally, KESIMPTA which is an EpiPen once a month.

I can tell you, I am feeling a little like a lab rat because I am now in secondary progressive as none of the drugs were able to slow the disease completely, and, sadly, my body is starting to feel these effects now.

I will explain a little more about this disease. It is the most surprising and unpredictable of diseases. Well, in my case, it is the disease that just keeps on giving. My first symptom was obviously my walking and loss of balance and motor skills. Fatigue is a huge part of MS and becomes a balancing act. I had always had trouble with my bladder, so next, I was referred to see a urologist, Professor Helen O'Connell, who also became my saviour, and her assistant, Dawn, who is the funniest person. I connect with her so well and love her humour.

The next step was to do urodynamics on my bladder, which meant going in and filling my bladder up with fluids to see how much it would hold before the urethra would release. My problem is the urethra wouldn't release, so if we couldn't do this, my bladder would keep filling until it pops. During my next conversation with Helen, she explained to me that I was going to have to start self-catheterising. I was very naïve about this whole situation because I knew nothing about it or where to start.

"Okay, so just for the next couple of days or a week I'll have to do this?" I asked. "No," she replied, "for the rest of your life." I then said, "What the fuck? Are you fucking serious?" Helen let out a breath, "I don't blame you for saying that, but yes, I am very serious." Next thing I knew, I had a continence nurse and I was learning how to put a catheter into my pee hole, which I'm telling you, isn't the easiest task to learn, especially because I'm guessing most women don't even realise where it is – aren't we lucky to have three holes?!

I had to try and hold a mirror so I could see what I was doing. That was ridiculous. I kept dropping it, so I just went by feel instead. Using catheters has its benefits, believe me. It meant I could make it to Melbourne without having to stop to go to the toilet three or four times. It all comes down to the fact that I couldn't empty my bladder properly. Imagine this: every time you stand up to go pee, you have to press down on your bladder and try and squeeze as much as you can out of the bladder three or four times, then repeat a couple of times. This is what I had to do every time.

If you can't empty your bladder properly, it leaves a little bit of urine in the bottom of your bladder, which can cause an infection. That's why I constantly had urinary tract infections. So now, I self-catheterise full time. I named them my piss sticks. You have to try and find the humour in every part of this disease, or it will eat you alive and take away everything, and I sure as hell wasn't going to let it rule my life. There was only enough room for one of us to be in charge and, yes, that was me... The other bonus is when drinking with friends, they have to pee all the time, especially once you break the seal. I can last for hours – sometimes all day!

Next on the agenda for symptoms, I have oscillopsia, a bouncing vision of the eyes. I had to see an ophthalmologist and a neuro ophthalmologist to get me on the right medication of clonazepam, three times a day, and gabapentin, up to eight times daily, also.

Hold on, there is more! I have two Keflex daily because of the catheters, to stop infection, and then baclofen three times daily, as a muscle relaxant, and then my monthly injection of KESIMPTA to try and slow progression. The biggest problem with taking all these tablets is you have to be organised, make sure you have all your scripts filled, and have enough on hand at all times.

So, a quick summary is that my legs don't work, they only have minimal feeling, and my eyes have to be controlled with medication, and, no, glasses don't work as it is a trauma to the eyes, pain, sensory feelings that cause spasms, slurred speech, sometimes and, yes, sometimes alcohol causes this!

I have Botox. I know what you are thinking, how good I look for my age?! Just jokes. I have it in my bladder to stop the urgency and to stop me pissing myself. I go to Melbourne twice a year to have this done. That's probably about a wrap – oh no, I have bowel issues too, so I have a gut health a specialist to control that. I also forgot my new symptom, which is hand cramping, so I can hardly hold a pen. Plus, now I choke when I drink because of the muscles in the neck. Fuck, I think myself lucky! Ha!

No two people with MS are the same. We all have different symptoms. I'm just lucky to have won the jackpot and got a hamburger with the lot. Hey, at least I'm still above the ground and not below it… I hope now some people have a better understanding of what this disease can cause.

Marnie & Charle in hospital

Fierce and Unstoppable

Catheter (piss stick)

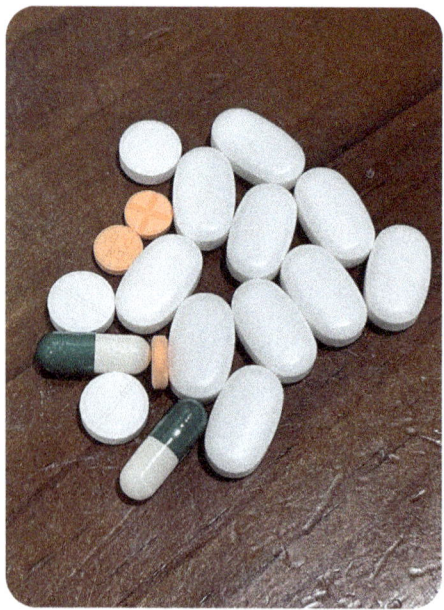

Daily pills

Medication

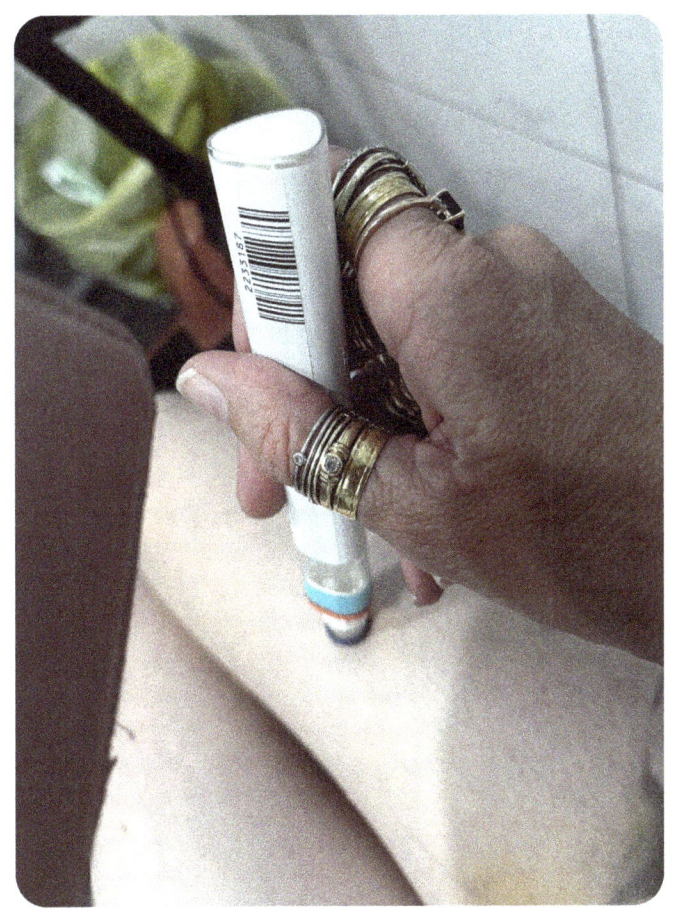

Monthly injection Kisempta

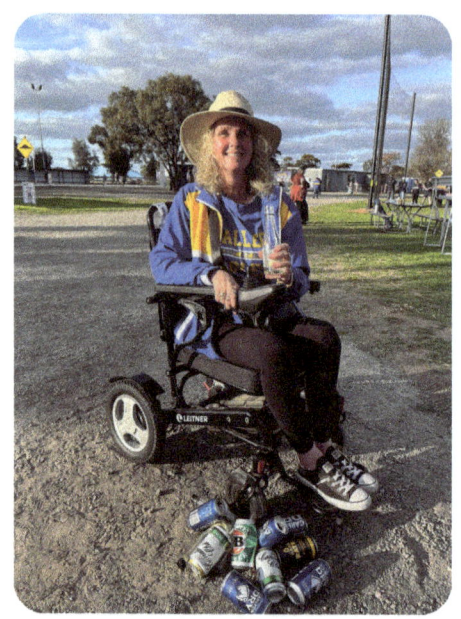

Charlie at footy 2025

Hayley, Josh & Charlie at Pink concert

Chapter 12:
Learning to Live with My Disability

"There's a future version of me who's proud I was strong enough."

Khanos

I have had this disease for going on almost 26 years now. That's over half of my life. My morning routine consists of waking up with my legs having spasms, so I stretch before I even move. I then have to try and move my legs to the side of the bed, grab hold of my cupboard, swing my legs around and sit up. This is not always an easy task because my legs are dead weight, and I can't move them all the time.

Once I'm up, next I have to take my tablets. These are the ones so that I can see, stop my spasms, and my antibiotic. Next, to the toilet to get undressed because I'm stable in there: I have grab rails all around. I clean my teeth, then to the shower, praying that I can stand up long enough to be able to use the soap, and then I can sit down on my chair. The next challenge is to stand up and dry myself. I then get back onto my scooter, which I park right beside the shower. I clean my face with wipes, then head to the walk-in wardrobe to pick out the clothes for the day, then back up to my bed.

I lift myself onto it to try and get dressed. This is a task on its own. Getting dressed is so hard and tiring. Sometimes I just want to sit and cry because something so simple shouldn't be so fucking hard. I am sure these are simple things that most people take for granted. I have

Charlie at Katrina's wedding

to allow myself an hour to get showered and dressed with my facial routine of moisturiser and perfume. Then finally, the shoes. Well, if you saw how I did this – putting one leg over my knee to try and put one on, then repeat to the other side. One last step: get back on my scooter and out into the lounge transfer to my other scooter so I can get outside to be picked up. Ah well, another day of success – the little things just to survive. But I'm all good now to start the day.

Fatigue plays a big part in this disease. It is frustrating being tired all the time and the smallest things take up so much energy. I don't drive anymore, which was probably the hardest thing for my independence to be taken away. The children made this decision once they found out I couldn't feel my feet to touch the pedals anymore and I was seeing double vision. It was a no-brainer, really. (Plus, there may have been

Learning to Live with My Disability

Charlie & Brian at home in the paddock

a couple of little mishaps in between, I know the ones who know about these are laughing and saying, "Do you think?!") This was really hard to come to terms with because now I really did have to rely on everyone to be picked up and dropped off. I have come to realise this is not entirely a bad thing, at least I never have to be designated driver.

It took a long time to learn how to cope, even though I had been doing it for a long time without even realising. The biggest thing is learning the limitations of what you can and can't do. This was my biggest problem because I like to go flat out all the time, and I didn't like to slow down. But there comes a time when your body makes you slow down, and you don't have a choice.

My body would relapse, then I would need another dose of steroids. That would pick me up for a while and I thought I was fine until you go, go, go, go – and the same thing happens again. It's just like repeat, repeat, repeat. So eventually, you have to learn the limitations, otherwise your body will stop completely. Learning to listen to your body is a very hard task, but it has to be done if you want to keep going.

I am extremely lucky that I have a huge circle of friends and family that I can lean on. But once again, my biggest fault is learning to ask for help. Once you learn how to actually do this, your life does become easier. My biggest fear is becoming a burden on everyone, especially my children. This is not what I want to happen. I want my children to live their lives and not be worrying every minute about their mother. I know they love me, and they want to try and help, but I've been very clear that when the day comes that I can't look after myself or feed myself, I don't want live like that anymore. As hard as it maybe for my children to hear, I don't want that kind of life for me or for them.

My wish is for them to go on, raise their families, be happy, and just remember that their mother was one of the strongest people they ever knew. If I can leave this kind of legacy behind for them to follow, I will be extremely happy. Hopefully, this won't happen for a very long time. I hate feeling useless and that I have to rely on everyone else to help me do everything. When you're very independent and stubborn, it takes a lot to actually ask for help.

Because I've always been so determined and positive, that's what has got me through this far, so to actually have to depend on everyone else to help you, it deflates your confidence to the bottom of the barrel. When you hit this low, it is hard to climb out, and this is when dark thoughts enter your mind, *Should I still be here? Do I want to still be here and put up with this struggle every day?*

But you have to try and shut this side off. Let it go blank and breathe and let resilience come through and say, *Hell, yeah! I'm not going anywhere! Who could possibly fill your rude, blunt, loveable shoes? You are one of a kind.* Well, that's what I tell myself…Yet once again, my adrenaline and determination kick in and decides, *Fuck this. I'm not going down without a fight.* I believe positive thinking is the key: if you can stay strong in your mind, then the rest of your body will follow.

I just have to mention, too, when Covid hit – I managed to avoid it for a long time, but in the end, it got me. I'm telling this story because it paralysed me. I rang Dr Booth, and he told me I had to be in hospital. He asked, "Do you want to ring the ambulance or me?" I said, "I will," which I didn't. He rang me later that afternoon and said, "Where are you?" I replied, "Oh, I'm still at home." He asked, "Can I talk to Brian, then?" And I said, "He has just stepped outside." He was working up the road.

Anyway, I was under instructions to drink 20ml of water every 20 minutes. I couldn't walk. Brian had to carry me to the toilet. I couldn't use my catheters because I couldn't hold it, so Brian had to do it. The poor bastard had to get down on his hands and knees and try and find the pee hole. He couldn't find it for ages and when he finally got it in, the poor bastard got covered in piss. Well, I guess that is true love for you. We still laugh about this.

Even after all these challenges, I'm not giving up. I have been put on this earth for a reason, and I have a purpose to inspire others to reach their full potential.

Josh & Charlie out at a function

Charlie & Hayley

Learning to Live with My Disability

Charlie

Chapter 13:
Constant Falls

"I am more vulnerable than I thought, but much stronger than I ever imagined"

Sheryl Sandberg

Every day, I wake up and wonder, *How many falls will I have today?* Just hoping I won't fall out of bed in the morning or in the middle of the night. It is very daunting not knowing whether you're even going to be able to get up and get out of bed. It is the unknown of this disease that is the part that worries me every day. If I know I'm going to fall, I just let it go. I don't try and brace myself, otherwise I'll end up with broken arms or wrists. I call it the "free fall" – less chance of hurting myself that way. It is definitely a worry.

Will I be able to take my tablets? Balance enough to get onto my scooter? Manage to get to the toilet on time? I constantly fall over in the shower because I sit there too long with the hot water just running over me. In my brain, it's telling me to get out but I just keep sitting there. I don't go anywhere without my phone anymore because I need to be able to have it to ring someone just in case. I usually have at least one fall a day or get stuck on the toilet, which I have had happen, and sat there at least an hour before someone come along to help. Sometimes I laugh; sometimes I cry.

I basically have Sarah on speed-dial. She doesn't live far from me, so I don't usually have to sit and wait very long until she gets there to pick me up. We do have a laugh when she does because of some of the

Charlie & Sarah

positions my body ends up in. Luckily, I'm double-jointed and things bend very easily. One day I had been on my reformer while I was waiting for Sarah to pick me up to take me to netball, I rang her and asked, "How far away are you?" She said, "I'm just coming through your gate. Why?" I said, "No reason. I'm just going to need you when you get in the door."

Sarah and her daughter walked in, and there I was, laying on the floor, laughing, because I tried to get off my reformer onto my scooter, and I missed and landed on the floor. They came, picked me up, and put me back on my scooter, and off we went. What a start to the day? This is not unusual, nearly an everyday occurrence, whether it be at home or at work. Once, when I fell in the shower, I didn't have my phone and I had no way of getting out. So I dragged myself along the carpet

Charlie & Hayley

and dragged my scooter behind me because I knew I would need it to be able to get back on it to move. Luckily, my upper body is quite strong, so I was able to pull myself up onto the bed after quite a few attempts, along with the determination that I wasn't going to be lying there all day.

After some carpet burn from dragging myself along – not what you are thinking – get your mind out of the gutter! – I got back on my scooter and got dressed. I felt this was a big achievement and felt very proud of myself to be able to have done this on my own. I can tell you that it's very tiring trying to lift your own body weight, especially when your legs don't work, and it also becomes very frustrating.

I have had many funny times when I had to try and get someone to pick me up, especially the day when the front door was locked and my nephew and friend had to come and break the lock on the door to be able to get in to get me. There I was lying naked, face down on the floor. We all still laugh about it. What else can you do? Like I said, if you don't laugh, you'll cry. I don't worry about people seeing me now with nothing on. It's just something that you have to get used to.

What's the old saying? Hang your pride up on the door and pick it up on your way out.

I don't usually hurt myself. I bounce very well, actually. Except one night, I wasn't so lucky. I had been asleep and when I woke up, I think I didn't have my bearings properly. I went to grab the back of my scooter and missed and fell. I thought I fell on my back, but I must've just rolled onto my back and had landed on my knee first. Luckily, my daughter and her boyfriend were home. They heard the crash as I hit my cupboard and the scooter, and they came running in to find me lying there.

They lifted me up so I could go to the toilet. Hayley was in there with me and said, "Are you okay, Mum? You don't look so good." I thought I was fine. My knee was very wobbly, but that's not unusual. So I just went and got back into bed until the next morning. When I went to get out of bed and stand up, I knew something was very wrong. It was the pain I had felt when I snapped my anterior cruciate in my knee many years before.

I have a very high pain tolerance, so I didn't worry about it too much until I went to see a physio and he said, "This is not good. You need to have an MRI." Bloody hell, what else could go wrong? The scan showed that I had broken my kneecap, bruised my bone, and torn my ligaments around the knee as well. I don't do things in halves – I always make sure I do a proper job. For about six weeks, it was bloody excruciating. I seriously would rather have gone through childbirth again than put up with that pain.

I decided to go and see a specialist to see exactly what I had done. I knew I wouldn't be able to have surgery because I wouldn't be able to do the rehab. I just needed to know the damage and how long it would take to recover. He told me it was a 12-week injury. I was about halfway through already, so I just had to put up with it. I kept walking on it the best I could, just getting around into my wheelchair and scooter. I don't know whether it was because I was older, but the pain was unbelievable, and the worst part? It was my fucking good knee on my good leg! It finally healed, but it still gives me trouble. I can't straighten it properly or put too much pressure on it. It gives out constantly. I need that leg! My other leg is stuffed enough as it is.

Anyway, onward and upward to see what else can be thrown at me. I have to wonder what it would be like to have normal legs again. I like to sit and people watch and see how people just take for granted that they can do all these things with their legs. I don't feel angry or jealous. I just feel amazed that people can still do this, and I can't, and never will be able to again. But that's okay. I have come to terms with that.

I knew when I first got diagnosed that there was a 50% chance that I would end up in a wheelchair. It took 20 years and now I'm there. I brag about how cool my wheels are in that at least I don't get tired, and I laugh while everyone else is running around feeling worn out and I'm as fresh as a daisy. You always have to make the best of things and sometimes being in a wheelchair has great perks, especially when you're at the airport when you get to go to the start of the line. We just wave as we go past.

All the girls know that whoever has taken me to the toilet knows that they're going to have to pull my pants down and pull them back up again, just while I try and balance. We do all laugh about this, especially the day when Sarah realised that I had put my undies on back-to-front. Oh, well, too late now. They are just going to have to stay that way!

Sarah, who is now one of my, carers is unreal. Every time I fall over, I ring her and she comes and picks me up off the floor, usually in the shower, but I could call her day or night, and she would always come. I call her to pick me up from work to do shopping or whatever I need. She's always there.

Charlie & Monica

Brian

Chapter 14:
Another Hospital Visit

"Looking out of a hospital window is different from looking out of any other. Somehow you do not see outside"

Carol Grace

Brian used to go to Bathurst every year for the car race with a bunch of mates on a bus. The kids were only young at this stage, but that was fine. I could cope no worries. At this stage, I could still walk. Though, that day, I started to feel unwell. I had been up early in the morning, organised veggies ready and had them peeled and cut up in the pot on the stove ready to cook for tea that night. Later in the day, I fell asleep in the chair while the kids were just playing on the floor with their toys. I had a friend turn up. She saw I was asleep, but then I heard the car door shut as she was leaving. I went out and told her to come back in. Monica knew I wasn't right but I said, "I'll be fine. I'm okay."

Later that night, I woke up shivering, freezing and cold, and I couldn't warm up. I needed to go to the toilet, but I couldn't get out of bed. My body wouldn't allow me to move. I started yelling out to Josh to try and wake him up. I needed to call someone. He was only five at the time and Hayley was only two. I just needed him to get me the phone so I could call someone to come and help me.

He got the phone, and I rang my mum, but she lived in Barham at the time. I couldn't speak anyway, so she couldn't really understand what was going on. I knew my body was shutting down. Josh had to ring the ambulance, which was a big task for a five-year-old. He stayed very calm and took his sister to the toilet. I remember that very clearly as he took her by the hand and helped her out of the room.

My mum had got off the phone and rang, Roberta, my mother-in-law who lived in Swan Hill, so she was able to get to home pretty quick. The ambulance had already arrived and were trying to work out how to get inside my house because at this stage we had a verandah all the way around: no ramps or easy doors for them to get in, so this was a bit of a challenge.

I was busting to go to the toilet. I just wanted them to put in a catheter so that I could relieve my bladder, but unfortunately, they are not allowed to do this. I had to wait until I got to the hospital. Luckily, Roberta had turned up because the kids weren't allowed to come in the ambulance with me. What a stupid rule. What would've happened if I had no one at home with them?

As I arrived at the hospital, so did Mum. They had sped from Barham to get there quickly. Mum later told me that when she had taken one look at me, I was as red as a tomato. I got taken in straight away. I begged them to relieve my bladder. Tests were done and found out that I had a really bad urinary infection. It was shutting my body down. I got started on antibiotics straight away through a drip. I was taken to the ward, put into a bed, and I think I passed out.

I just remember my body being so sore. They said it was from all the shivering from the infection. I woke up with Brian standing beside me at my bed. They had got in touch with them while he was away and made sure they got home as early as they could. I had never been so glad to see him in all my life. Dr Booth came around. I told him I didn't want to stay in hospital. I'm very impatient like that. I wanted to go home, so he gave me very strong antibiotics to take with me and discharged me.

Another Hospital Visit

I was unaware that a urinary infection could do that to your body. Food for thought, people: don't let it get that bad. Just a few little tips that can hopefully help someone – I didn't even know I had the infection. I usually can tell by burning, but there are other symptoms that you can think about in the future. If your urine smells bad, that's a dead giveaway, so get onto it quickly. Sometimes you might think you have an infection, but it might be something called cystitis, which has the same symptoms, but get onto the Ural, a sachet to mix in water, and that will fix that problem quite quickly. Plus, drink plenty of water.

This was the first of many visits to hospital to come, but by far the scariest. I was so proud of my kids. They just took it in their stride for such little ones. Hospital life was something I had to get used to. I've now seen the inside of so many hospitals; it's just like second nature. I'm what you call a frequent flyer…

Gus, Charlie & Maria

Chapter 15:
A Wedding In 45° Degree Heat

"If you don't know how to say no, your body will say it for you through physical illness"

Dr Gabor Mate

Just in February, I had Julie's daughter's wedding. I had my hair done, bought a new dress, and was all ready to go and enjoy some great company and have some fun. But I was not prepared for what happened. I stepped outside and it was extremely fucking hot! I thought I would be fine. My body is different from the majority of people who have MS. Most MS sufferers like the cold weather, but I'm the opposite. I hate the cold and love the heat.

That day was different. It was 45° degrees with no breeze, and it was extreme heat. I still thought once I got there and had a wine in my hand I would cope, but my body had other ideas of what it would do. We got through the ceremony, and I thought, *If I can just cool my body temperature down, I will be okay.* I had Glenda (or Fluffa as I call her) pouring bottles of water down my back and front, putting ice in my bra and all over my body. I couldn't even hold a glass of wine or a bottle of water to drink. She was having to hold it up, so I could drink it. I was devastated – I couldn't even drink. This was a very sad and rare occasion.

I tried to have something to eat, but nothing would work. All I could think was, *Fuck my body*. For once in my life, I really hated it. Someone

Charlie before wedding

mentioned there was a pool there. I was quite happy to strip my dress off and someone throw me in, but we weren't allowed near it. Next, I tried to move over near the bar where I thought there was a little bit of shade, but this didn't help either. All of a sudden, I thought I was going to throw up. Hayley was waitressing at the wedding, and she took one look at me and said, "Mum, you are not okay." I had also realised this, so I asked a couple of the girls whether someone could

A Wedding In 45° Degree Heat

please take me home. I just needed to get out of there. This had never happened to my body before ever.

They pulled the car around so I could go over to it. It was like I had an army of people around me to get me to the car. Once I had reached the car, thank God Hayley was there to lift me in because, by this stage, I couldn't even speak. I was nearly passed out. My body was shutting down from the heat. I was driven home by great friends, Menina and Billy. I didn't realise another group had followed them in the car behind.

By the time I got home, Josh and my nephew, Marcus, were there waiting. Hayley had already rung them and told them to get home. I was very pleased to see them because I knew that my Marcus would be able to just lift me out of the car, onto my scooter, and then throw me into my bed. Fluffa was in the car behind with her husband, Shaun, and Gus.

I was very pleased Fluffa was there. She came and stripped me off, put my nightie on, gave me a drink of water, and tucked me in. The boys had turned on the air-conditioner right up so my body temperature could be cooled down quickly. Once it happened, I was fine. Although it was a big wake-up call to me that I didn't realise just how quickly my body could shut down. It was a bit scary. Once again, it just showed how great my friends are and how much they care about me.

Later on, I had a visit from all the girls: Hayley; my niece, Milla; Ella; and Hope. They were all waitressing at the wedding and saw what had happened. They were all worried, so they come to check on me to make sure I was okay, which I thought was very sweet.

So, it was a lesson learned: my body isn't invincible and, once again, I need to learn my limitations. This is a very hard task for me because I still love to be social and enjoy everything; I don't like to miss out. But unfortunately, sometimes you just need to think about your body and put your health first, even if it means missing out.

Dee, Sarah, Charlie & Maree at footy 2024

Chapter 16:
Living with MS

"Life isn't about waiting for the storm to pass; it's about learning to dance in the rain."

Vivian Greene

Now, if I stop and think what my life has become, it revolves around making sure I have medication so that I can see to stop the bouncing vision, antibiotic so I don't get urinary infections, try and control spasms. To do this, I have to take up to 20 tablets a day just to keep my body functioning. Then I must give myself an injection once a month just to try and slow the progression. I have to use catheters just to be able to pee, I have to use enemas to empty my bowel before I go out anywhere, then take tablets to block me up again, just to make sure I don't have an accident This all has to take place just so I can go out in public. I have to go to Melbourne twice a year just to put Botox in my bladder, so I don't piss myself.

This disease has taken away my independence because I can't drive anymore; I need carers now which I never thought I would need, but I do, because of all the falls. Plus, I can't cook anymore. A lot of the time if I'm home alone, it's just easier not to eat. Unbelievably, the hunger passes. Eating is overrated. Please, no offence to my carers, they are fantastic and there for my safety but having people in your house is hard to get used to. Sometimes I am happy with my music and my own company, that way I can cry whenever I feel like it. But it takes pressure off my children and friends if I have carers with me. I want my children to be just that, not my carers. They didn't sign up for that. I mean, seriously, at their age who the fuck wants to be looking after their disabled, useless mother?

At times, I feel like MS has stolen my life and I am a burden on everyone involved in it. I'm stuck in a wheelchair or a scooter, even to get around my own house. Some days I have very dark thoughts about whether or not I really want to be here. I apologise to a couple of friends when I feel this way. Sometimes I have expressed to them what I would like to do. When you're alone, you have a lot of time on your hands to think about things and whether or not you really do want to end your life. Every thought goes through your brain about how you can do it. As I said, my brain never stops, so I have a lot of scenarios running through it constantly.

But then I think of what I would be leaving behind. I couldn't do it to my children, family, and friends, so I snap out of it. I have been talked off the ledge a few times by a couple of friends. Then I realise, *I am strong and I have too much to live for.* I was given this disease and everything it throws at me because I can handle it. I'm not going to lie down and let it beat me. No way. Who the hell could replace my mouth and personality?

I don't want to sound like I am full of myself. That's not the case. I just want you to realise you can have dark thoughts, but you can also have fantastic ones; you can have dreams that you can make come true. You just have to believe in yourself. It takes a lot of energy to do this, but with resilience and determination, you will get there. Bet on yourself, rely on your friends and family, and you will come through the other side. I am living proof of that.

My latest symptom is my hands cramping with tonic spasms, which are also a rare symptom. Once again, lucky me, I'm going for a record. I think I can't even hold a pen anymore to write, or if I do, it looks like chicken scratch or like a one-year-old has written it. My neurologist has no answers for this except to try and take more medication to relax the muscles and, hopefully, the cramping will let go. Sometimes it works; sometimes it doesn't. Just another hurdle to jump over. It's okay, just a bump in the road that I will learn to live with and get over.

I saw my neurologist not long ago. He gave me news which I was expecting. It's just different to be told what you were thinking anyway. Although it was worse than what I expected, he told me that my spine is completely covered in lesions now. It's completely white, so if I have a scan, he can't even tell me if there has been any more damage because he can't see my spine anymore. I just sat there and then said, "Okay. Well, what is my next stage?" He answered, "There is no next stage, Charlie. This is it. You are in the last stage now."

If my daughter hadn't been with me, I probably would've burst into tears, but amazingly, I held it together. Well, what do I do now? Make the most of what I've got. He told me to travel now, while I still can. So that is my plan: see as much of Australia as I can and then go overseas again next year. At this stage of my life, I did stop and think, *What do I have left to live for?* My answer to myself was **plenty**.

I can still talk, get around, and enjoy my life to its fullest, and that is what I'm going to do. Like I said, I'm not going to sit and let some shitty disease rule my life. I'm going to take charge and do what I want to do… This is where the power of the mind takes over and you find strength in every ounce of your body. I'm trying to exercise and keep my strength up so that I can keep transferring from my chair and my scooter and into cars, which I have to be lifted into. I want to be able to achieve the best that the world has left to offer me.

I will keep drinking my Moscato, laughing, working, and socialising as much as I possibly can. I've told myself this diagnosis is only words and I am a strong, determined, and stubborn bitch – and there is no way I'm going down without a fight.

The worst part about when I saw my neurologist last was that he works out of the Alfred hospital, which was where Brian passed away. We went down to the cafeteria afterwards, and it brought back terrible memories of when we were sitting there and my husband was in the ICU, dying. I was very glad to get out of there, back in the car, and on our way home. The trip home was a long one, but I did do a lot of thinking – once again, coming to terms with the news I had just been given. Sometimes I feel like my body has been dragged through the ringer repeatedly, but it seems to keep surviving. I asked Hayley, "How do I cope now?" She replied, "It's okay, Mum. You have an army around you."

My final message about MS is that it will only control you if you let it, and I have no intentions of letting it win. As I've said previously, I don't like to lose, so I'm not about to start now.

Fuck you, MS!
I will fight for me – CANI (song)

Part 3:
Losing Brian

Chapter 17:
The Day It Happened

"We walk this earth for time that we are given until we return to it."

J R R Tolkien

Firstly, I'm going to start off by telling you what happened step-by-step that day. I have a photographic memory, so it plays through my brain like a video every day. Believe me, this is not something that you want to relive every day, but once again, it's just how my brain works overtime.

The Beginning Of The End

Friday 29th July 2022 – Day 1

For some unknown reason, I woke up about 3am in a fright, sat straight up in the bed, and knew something was wrong. I put my hand on Brian to feel him. He was warm, so I thought everything was okay. I rolled over and went back to sleep. He got out of bed early, as normal, and went to work.

Hayley was dropping me off on her way to school. I got out of her ute and onto my scooter. As I was driving my scooter into the office, I was going too fast, and I hit a corner on a pack of plaster. Brian said, "Bloody hell. I've got to sell them now!" He laughed. Hayley had her window down as she was driving off and I heard her yelling, "You are a dickhead, Mum!"

We went into the office to start our day. Brian sat on the bench, as he normally did, and we started talking. Then Jika (Alan) turned up, as he usually did, just for a chat. Next, my mum and Bill turned up just out of the blue. I didn't know they were coming. They were standing in the showroom on the other side of the counter. Jika was standing next to Brian, near the filing cabinet, and they were talking fine. Brian was talking bullshit, as usual. He took a phone call from Josh to see what he wanted for smoko…

And that's when it all began.

Brian was leaning on the filing cabinet, talking normally, and the next thing, he started falling towards Jika. Jika said, "Are you all right, mate? What's going on?" He tried to catch Brian as he was falling towards him, but he couldn't stop him. Brian landed on the floor and started having seizures. We were all alarmed. Mum and Jika both told me to ring an ambulance straight away, which I tried to do, but I think I was in disbelief.

I got put through to an operator who wasn't based here. It's wherever the fuck it was – Ballarat or something like that – which is fucking ridiculous because they had no idea where we were. I was trying to give the address, but it wasn't coming up on the computer. I started screaming and swearing, "For fuck's sake! It's Hovendens Plaster Works. We are just around the corner from you. How the fuck can you not know where we are?"

They kept asking me questions. *Was he breathing? What noises was he making?* I'm trying to relay these questions over to Jika because I was on the phone and I didn't know what he was doing. Mum decided to ring the ambulance herself because I was too angry and upset to even speak to them to give Jika instructions on what to do. He started resuscitation on him straight away.

I hung up the phone and rang Bob, "Get to the shed straight away." He tried to ask why I was yelling. I said, "Just get here, now." As all this was taking place, Josh walked through the door with his smoko in a box to see his dad lying on the ground. He dropped the box and went to run towards him. I stopped him and yelled, "Go and get the fucking ambulance. They're not coming. It's been too long." He ran out the door and got in the ute. Poor Eli was chasing him up the road as Josh took off.

Josh got to the ambulance station, and it was all locked up. A couple of ladies came across the road to tell him that two ambulances and a car had just left. Josh returned to the shed, but he still got back before the ambulance. I knew the next thing I needed to do was to ring the school and get Hayley to the shed or she would never forgive me if she had never got to see her father again.

As Bob had ran out of the shop, Kylie knew something was wrong, so she followed him. I had rung them because I knew I needed to have Bob there for Josh and Kylie there for Hayley.

Finally, after what seemed like an eternity, the ambulance arrived. As they were walking through the door, I heard them on the walkie-talkie saying the chopper was 50 minutes away. This was not a good sign, so they obviously knew things were bad. To their credit, they worked very quickly. There were five of them. They dragged Brian away from the doorway, just a little bit, so they could work on him. All I could do was sit in my office chair and watch. They pumped so much adrenaline into him. They kept working on him with resuscitation until they finally got his heart beating again.

Bob had rung his brother, and they were all there, just watching through the glass. Bob told Josh all he wanted to do was smash the glass and lift me out of there, but I wouldn't have left him anyway. I remember just sitting and watching, with my hands on my head, thinking, *What the fuck is happening?* Hayley was in the showroom with Kylie and Carinda, watching from that side of the glass. Carinda drove Hayley from school to work, thank God.

I have tears streaming down my face while I'm writing this and having a drink while I'm telling this story. It's traumatic to even relive it this way. I thought seeing it in my head every day was bad enough.

Next, they were loading him onto a stretcher. Kylie was helping them as they got him ready to put into the ambulance and take him out to the airstrip. We all followed to see him off in the chopper. I still feel sorry for Eli because we all just took off and left him there on his own, but someone had to man the shed. Brian would've been so proud of him for doing that because that was his main priority.

We all headed out to the airstrip, and the chopper was there waiting. We went out onto the tarmac, and in doing so, the ambos called me over, and they lowered Brian's stretcher down so I could give him a kiss goodbye, not knowing that this would be the last time he would be here, although I think I knew, in my heart, that he was gone already.

They were flying him to Bendigo because they thought it was a heart attack. The kids took a video of him flying off in the chopper because we thought we'd be able to show him how much of a fuss he had been making. We all left and went home to pack a bag. Bob wanted to drive us and Josh was going to follow.

When I got home, I had to make some phone calls because typical Swan Hill – the beauty of a small town – everybody knew something was wrong because of all the ambulances parked out the front of work. The only thing was everyone thought it was me, which made sense. But it was Brian.

Hayley drove us around to Bob's and then he drove and started heading towards Bendigo with Josh behind us in his car. None of us spoke on the drive. I mean, what do you say? We were all in shock. This was until I got a phone call on our way to Bendigo. It was the hospital telling us to keep heading to Melbourne because it wasn't a heart attack. It was a bleed on the brain, an aneurysm.

Bob will laugh at this because he thinks this part of the story is hilarious, and it actually was. Afterwards, we all laughed. The lady on the phone was telling me about Brian. She was trying to prepare me for what we needed to know, in doing this, she told me that treating Brian's injury was going to be quite expensive. I started screaming, "I don't give a fuck how much it costs. I'll sell my house if I have to!" She then went on to say, "I think you misheard me. I didn't say 'expensive'. I said 'extensive.'" *Well, fuck.*

I apologised immediately because I felt like a real arsehole. Bob and Hayley didn't know what was going on. I got off the phone and explained that I had misheard her that she had said "extensive" not "expensive". Bob burst out laughing, then so did me and Hayley. This is when you'll find we tried to find humour in every part, even at the worst time in our lives. We all still have a good chuckle about this, especially Bob. It's his favourite story to tell about this shitty situation.

Also, on the way, I rang my neurologist, Helmut, on the way down and asked him what Brian's chances were. He said, "It doesn't look good." I never told anyone that news. I just kept it to myself.

We arrived in Melbourne after dark and then had to try and find some accommodation. That was nearly impossible, but we did eventually find a dodgy place. It was a bed and a shower, and that was all we needed. There was no point us going to the hospital that night as we weren't sure exactly where he was at that stage, so we thought we would just leave it and go there first thing in the morning.

Saturday 30th July – Day 2

Unfortunately, this was all happening through the Covid period, so we weren't allowed in until they had got Brian's results back to make sure that he was Covid-free. He was being treated at the Alfred Hospital, which was the best place for him to be. That was where Helmut worked out of too.

We went and waited at Roberta's until we got a call from the hospital to let us in to see him. I rang Sonia to try and find us some accommodation close to the hospital as I didn't know Melbourne at all or where anything was close to there, anyway. I was very thankful for her to be organising this for me I also asked her to let all the girls know. It was one less thing I had to worry about.

When we finally got into the hospital, we had a hurdle to cross, which become one of many. As Brian was in the ICU, they had a stupid fucking rule that if you weren't 18, you weren't allowed in. Hayley only had about three weeks to go before her 18th birthday, and so she wasn't quite of age. Oh my God, this was just one of many times that these nurses were going to see my temper rage. I spoke to one nurse, and she said, "It's not possible there's nothing I can do. I can't let her in." I said, "Well, I suggest you put your supervisor on the phone." She replied, "I am the supervisor." I then went on to suggest in a not-quite-so-nice manner that she better find someone higher up, "Otherwise I'm going to scream the roof off this fucking hospital if you do not let my daughter in to see her father!" She relented and let her in.

I spoke to the doctor in charge, and the next thing I knew, there was another doctor there saying, "I'm here to give permission for the child to be let in the room." I grabbed Hayley and said, "Here she is." The doctor looked confused, "But she isn't a child?" I said, "Thank you. Exactly my fucking point."

The Day It Happened

I am telling you now, there is no possible way that they would've been able to keep Hayley out of there. Hell would freeze over before I would have allowed that to happen. As most people know, my temper has a very short fuse and being put in that situation – it was even shorter. As I said, there were many obstacles to cross throughout our short visit in this hospital. The next one was only two people were allowed in the room at the same time. I couldn't even be in there at the same time with both my children. When they told us this, I had to get some air. I was about ready to blow my stack again.

It was very confronting walking into that room for the first time and seeing my husband lying there with a tube coming out the top of his head, draining blood, another tube down his throat. I tried to make light of the situation to one of the nurses and made a joke, "Bloody hell, there's not even any plaster in that blood. I can't believe it." She just looked at me and had no idea what the fuck I was going on about. I mumbled under my breath, "Oh, for Christ's sake. Get a fucking sense of humour!" We spent all day there and then went back to the motel to have a drink. But in Melbourne, they only serve shit beer and drinks. I swear to God, the country is seriously the best place to live.

We had to go shopping to get a few things as we had packed lightly not expecting to stay this long. We needed more clothes as there was nowhere to wash them. We were also trying to find somewhere to get some photos developed. They suggested putting photos around the hospital room. Sometimes that helped with the patient, but we couldn't find anywhere. They also suggested playing music. This also sometimes helped to spark movement. As we were only allowed two in the room at a time, two of us sat in the room while two sat in the car on FaceTime and played this song, *End of the Line*. We all swear to God that we saw his eyes flicker when this music started playing, so at this stage, we still had hope.

Sunday 31st July – Day 3

We got up in the morning and had some breakfast, meanwhile I got a phone call from the doctor just with an update. We were told we needed to decide as a family– because even if Brian did come through this, he would have been unresponsive and wouldn't have been able to feed or do anything for himself again.

As I delivered this news to Bob and the children, Bob said straight away, "No, he's not living like that. He always said when we were all working in the old folks' homes, 'If I ever get to that stage, pull the plug.'" We were all in agreement. There was no way he would ever want to live that way, our hearts sank at this thought. We therefore went on to make some phone calls to the family, that if they wanted to say goodbye, they needed to get to Melbourne ASAP.

Then we headed back to the hospital and sat in hope that he would open his eyes. When they were doing the neurological testing on him, we were praying that he would respond in some way that would at least give us a little glimmer of hope that he was going to make it through this. The doctors were very upfront and told us they had tried to go in and clamp the bleed again, but it didn't work. There was too much blood, and they couldn't see exactly where the bleed was.

After another long day at the hospital, it was back to the motel to have more drinks. This time, we were doing shots. Marnie came to the motel that night to have drinks with us and just to be there as support. Danny and Jacinta, Brian's favourite cousins, who lived at Glen Waverley also came. We had spent a lot of time with them. Danny was more like a brother to Brian than a cousin.

The boys explained the situation about the beer, so Danny smuggled in some Carlton Dry in a Safeway cloth bag so no one could see. The boys just poured the stubbies into the glasses. They had to be sneaky, away from the bar staff. It was nice to have some family and friends around with us at this very difficult time in our lives. I said to Bob, "So, when are you going home? What are your plans?" He turned to me and said, "I'm not going anywhere. I have to drive you home." We all would've been lost without Bob, Brian's baby brother, who he loved very much.

Cracks were beginning to appear to us that the chance Brian may not make it. I was trying to stay strong for my kids. Hayley was sleeping with me in the bed at the motel, just hugging me throughout the night, I think we both knew, deep down, what the outcome was going to be.

Monday 1st August – Day 4

My phone rang at about 7am. It was the doctor. I jumped out of bed. I was hoping for good news. But instead, this became the worst day of our lives. The doctor explained we needed to come into the hospital straight away. I rang Bob and Josh and told them the news. We all jumped in the shower quick as we possibly could to get there. When we got to the hospital, we had to wait to see the doctors, but this took hours.

When the doctor was finally ready to speak to us, they took us upstairs onto another floor and we walked past rooms. It looked like a morgue. They took us into a room where they had monitors set up to do teleconferences because Bob's wife Kylie and his brothers were on their way. Making our way into this room, we all knew what it meant because there were chairs and a table. On the table were boxes and boxes of tissues.

The monitors were set up so that the boys and Kylie could listen to what the doctor was about to tell us. He waited till everyone was ready. He asked the boys to pull over and stop driving. We disconnected Kylie because she had the girls in the car, and we didn't think they needed to hear that news until they were with us.

When we were ready, the doctor delivered the news that Brian had passed away during the night. Although his brain was dead, his heart was still beating, so we still had to turn off the monitor.

I was completely numb.

The children cried, along with Bob and his mother. I couldn't stand to be in the room any longer, and I still feel guilty about this – that I left the room and went down to be with Brian. I just left my children there. What sort of mother does that? But I couldn't cope. I needed to be with him.

I went downstairs to his room and just held his hand and cried. I rang Marnie while I was in there and all I could manage to tell her was that he was gone. I put my head on his tummy and hugged him. My heart had shattered into a million pieces that can never be put back together again.

After I had had my time with him, I pulled myself together and then rang the children. I told them they needed to come down and say goodbye to their father. I think this is possibly the hardest thing I had ever had to do: sit and watch, while my children cried at their father's side. As we slowly made our way out of the room, it was time for Bob and Roberta to go in and see Brian. While they were doing this, the rest of the family arrived. Kylie, Milla, Miah, Steve, Darren, and Marcus. As luck would have it, my brother, Paul, had flown into Melbourne that morning so he also made his way to the hospital to be with us. They all took turns going in and saying their goodbyes. The boys found it very confronting and couldn't stay in the room very long.

Would you believe it? I had another confrontation with the reception staff, this time because they weren't going to let Milla and Miah in because they weren't 18. Well, this time there was no filter at all. The receptionist copped absolutely everything that I had to offer. I don't think she would ever have heard the language that came out of my mouth that day.

It didn't stop there. The abuse came out of my mouth like lava out of a volcano.

The nurses had to pull me aside and put me in a little room to try and calm me down. But there was no calming down at this stage. Paul sat in with me, just as some support, as I unleashed again. I look back and think it wasn't pretty, but anyway, *Fuck it*. I had nothing left to lose.

They gave us a room for all of us to sit in while we all took turns of going back in to see Brian, but to tell us that we couldn't stay in that room the whole time because it was supposed to be for all the families. We didn't care. We just stayed in there anyway.

The doctor approached me one more time and we had to go back into the fucking room again. This time they wanted to talk to us about organ donations. I asked the family what their thoughts were. Bob said, "Well, if it can help someone else…" Josh was undecided, as was I. But Little Miss Hayley made the decision for all of us. She piped up and said, "NO. My father doesn't share anything, so he's not sharing his organs." She was correct. Brian never shared his food with the children or with anyone. He never shared anything. So the decision was made.

The doctor looked at me as if to say, *Are you really serious about this?* My answer to him was, "No, we are not donating his organs. If we are not all in agreement, it is not happening." They kept trying to pressure us, but I stood strong and kept saying, "No." I do remember asking, "So when can I take him home?" They looked at me strangely, but I was deadly serious. So I asked again, "When can I take my husband home?" I knew I just needed to get him home.

It was getting late and we were all really tired, but they had to ask one more question: when did we want to turn the machine off? They said we could have him ready in a couple of hours. Bob, thank God, said, Can I please bring them back in the morning? We are just all so tired and want to leave." It had been a very emotional and draining day for everyone.

We all left the hospital and headed back to the motel. We had to try and get extra rooms for everyone, and thankfully the motel was very accommodating. Now, this is a funny moment that I remember about Bob. They had changed his room so he could be with his family, but as he went to get in the room, there was someone else in there. He came downstairs into the foyer, where we were all sitting with all his clothes in his hands, carrying on about the room. I couldn't stop laughing. Like I said, if you don't laugh, you cry.

Now came the hard part: ringing everyone and tell them that Brian had passed away. Hayley came up to me and said, "It's okay, Mum. I'll do it. I'll ring Grandma, Poppy, Sam, Lisa, Mon, Brad and some other friends." I couldn't believe how strong she was to be able to do that. She was only 17.

I rang Ernie and Peter. I knew by telling these good friends that they would then ring everyone else that needed to know. Once again, the beauty of the Bush Telegraph: the whole town would soon know the news.

We all sat around that night together, drank, and shared stories about that wonderful man that had been taken away from us way too soon.

Tuesday 2nd August – Day 5

We fronted up to the hospital for one last time. It was just Bob, Kylie, the girls, Hayley and me. We were waiting out the front for Josh. I rang him and said, "Where are you?" He said, "I'm at Calder already. I can't do it." I said, "That's okay." I never wanted either of the kids to do anything they weren't comfortable with. "You just keep going." I said, "I'll see you at home."

We made our way into the ICU room for the last time. The nurse actually asked us whether we would like photocopies of Brian's hand. We answered and said, "That would be lovely. Thank you." I was extremely grateful for this, just to have one final part of him. Hayley, Bob, and I made our way into the room where they had a TV set up. That meant we could play music to him for one last time.

Bob ended up leaving the room. He couldn't handle it either, so that just left Hayley and me. The nurse removed the tube while we watched. We then went on to play him a couple of songs for the last time: *Bed of Roses* by Bon Jovi and then *End of the Line* by the Traveling Wilburys. After these songs had finished, we then let the nurse know we were ready for her to turn the machine off. Hayley and I had said our goodbyes for one last time and then we stood either side of him, holding his hand, just waiting for his heart to stop beating.

I was actually surprised at how long it took before it does actually stop. It's not like on the movies where the flat line happens instantly; that's what I was expecting. But it took what felt like a very long time. Once it had stopped, the nurse come and told us that he was officially gone. She also told us that we were welcome to stay the whole day with him if we liked, I turned to her and said, "Please don't take this the wrong way, but we just need to get the fuck out of here now." We left the room and went to meet up with Bob, Kylie, and the girls, where we all hugged each other and cried.

Bob drove us home, but none of us really spoke. I did have to make another couple of phone calls on the way. I have never felt so empty in all my life. Leaving that place and leaving him behind it just felt wrong.

When we finally got home and walked inside the house, it made me feel sick to the stomach that he wasn't there. I was sad. I was so fucking angry. I went into my room, and with my arm, I just knocked everything off my bedside table onto the floor in one swift action of my arm.

Our whole world had been ripped apart and torn to shreds. There was a hole in my heart and soul that had just been stolen for no possible reason and without explanation. Nothing would ever be the same again.

Although, in some ways, it was if he knew that he made sure that the house was finished for me. The bathroom and kitchen had been renovated and made accessible. Then the concrete outside had been finished, along with the ramps and rails.

He had always told the kids that if something happened to him, they were to look after their mother no matter what. He was very serious about this, because this as much as he loved his children, which was a lot, I was his whole world. He made sure that I came first for everything.

Josh, Charlie & Hayley at Lalbert ball 2025

The Day It Happened

Brian at home

The Chevs before the funeral

Chapter 18:
The Funeral

"Be grateful for every second of every day you get to spend with the people you love. Life is so precious"

Helen Barry

Planning Brian's Funeral

After we had got home, the flowers started arriving. My house looked like a florist. There were so many flowers, and they just kept coming. We would go somewhere, come home and there would be more flowers at the gate because no one could get in with the three Blue Heelers in the yard. We joked that if Brian had been alive, he would've set up a table out the front, selling the flowers on. I had probably a week at home because of all the visitors that kept calling in. Hayley was with me, but Josh had to go straight back to work, which in hindsight, was probably a good thing to keep his mind busy.

Almost as soon as I got home, I had to ring Raelene O'Halloran, director, to start organising . We all worked together to make this happen with Bob and Kylie to help us. We tried to keep the humour up to help us get through it. As Hayley and I pulled up to parlour, it was dark and she asked, "Can I park here? Will anyone mind?" I replied, "I don't think there's going to be too many coming out to argue with us from here, Hayley, so I think we'll be fine," and we both laughed.

We sat down and Raelene started asking questions. The first question was, "Do you have a plot?" I looked at her, dumbfounded, and said,

"No, why the fuck would I already have a plot?!" She soon got used to my language and our warped sense of humours. We asked whether we could take Brian in his coffin in the back of the Chevy pick-up Ute. At first, she was hesitant but then agreed. We needed to put sockets in the back so that we would be able to tie the coffin down tight. Bob and OP took care of this.

It was only a couple of days before Brian had passed when he said to Josh, "If something ever happens to me, I want to be taken out in the back of the Chevy in the Ute." Josh replied, "Don't you want to go in the back of the wagon?" Brian quickly responded, "No, I want to go in the fresh air." Once again, it was as if he knew. Why else would he bring this up now?

Bob went on to ask Raelene, "Do you think if we backed up to the hole that we have to put him in and just slam on the brakes, do you reckon we could land him in there?" We burst out laughing! Once again, our warped sense of humour. We had to hand over all the photos collected for the visual at , and then we had to pick out all the songs for the church and the cemetery that we wanted to play.

We chose to start with *It's a Long Way to the Top* by ACDC. It was good having us all there together because we all had an input and everyone agreed. There were to be no readings as we were not religious at all – and that would be the last thing that Brian wanted. I had decided to do the eulogy along with Hayley. We picked the flowers that we wanted on top of the coffin and then everything that sat on top were his treasured memories. There had to be a photo of his puppies, his three Blue Heelers, who were his pride and joy, along with his red plaster bucket and all his old tools in it that he had for years and years.

God, there was so much to organise and think about. We also had to pick out a coffin. We looked through books, but I couldn't do

Ernie's hot rod with photos of Brian on doors

this. So, Hayley (the strong little bugger) and Aunty Kylie went to parlour to do this. We nearly buried him with his wedding ring, but Raelene advised us against it. Thank goodness! I now wear it on my chain around my neck every day. While they were there, Briany arrived in the hearse to the parlour. A bit freaky for them – he must have just been making sure they picked out something comfy for him!

When I was writing his eulogy, I kept recording things on my phone as I thought of them. I then sat with Hayley, and she typed it up on her laptop. Once all this was done, the boys organised all the old cars, and all his mates were organised to ride their Harleys on the day.

The night before , we had the viewing. I had never been to one, before so the thought of going to see my husband for the very last time didn't seem right. The kids came, along with Brian's brothers, my dad, and a friend of his, Terry. Hayley also brought along Diesel, his dog, who was very, very well-behaved. He just sat there, and he even watched the visual. It was like he knew. They say dogs are very intuitive to this sort of thing, and now I believe it.

Firstly, I have to say thanks to my dad because he dressed Brian in his clothes and got him ready. We put him in his work clothes, which consisted of his Hovendens work shirt, his navy work pants, sunnies on his head, and his work glasses that clicked together around his neck – he never took those off – and, last but not least, his beloved Crocs.

To Dad's credit, he made him look just like him. As you can imagine, this was extremely emotional for all of us. We all had our time with him to say goodbye. I gave him a kiss, but his body was so cold. I wasn't expecting that. Though, I suppose they have to keep the body in the fridge, don't they?

As we were leaving, we realised we hadn't put a trowel in with him or a can of his favourite beer, Carlton Light. His two nephews, Michael and Marcus, went back to the shed and got them, brought them back to Raelene and put them in the coffin with him. Thank you, boys.

The Funeral

Friday 12th August 2022

The day of the funeral, we all got up and got dressed, ready for the worst day of our lives: burying the most important person in our lives. It all seemed like a really bad dream. Of course, in true Brian style, nothing went to plan. The Ute wouldn't start, and all his brothers were out there trying to get things going. I was in the Ute with Josh. Hayley

The Funeral

was driving Brian's Hilux; Bob was in the wagon with his family; Marcus drove his van. We wanted all his vehicles there.

And typically, one of the Harleys wouldn't go, so the boys were running up the road in their suits, trying to push start it, but anyone who knew Brian knew this was something that he would be laughing about because it's very typical of him for nothing to be working on time.

As we are good friends with the Pickerings, they had organised for our truck, that has our signwriting on the side of it, to be parked right near the grain shed where the service was being held so that everyone could see it as they pulled in to park. I knew his funeral would be huge when we got there. The cars and people that were there – it was truly overwhelming at the number of people who came to pay their respects.

When we arrived, we were ushered off to a room at the side while they waited for everyone to come in and for us to all be ready. I can't explain what I was feeling that day because I think we were all running on adrenaline to get us through this horrible day. I think I was numb, and everything was a blur. Not everything was registering, but I knew I had a job to do and I had to stand strong for my children. There was time to break later, but not in this moment.

It was time. They were taking us into the church, ready to be seated at the front. It was very daunting because the coffin was right in front of where we were sitting. That was pretty hard to swallow, thinking that he was just lying there inside. As everyone was seated, the celebrant started with a little bit and then Hayley and I were called up to do our part. As I was on the stage in front of the microphone, I was staring down at Brian's coffin. Never in my wildest dreams did I think I would ever have to deliver this speech. I couldn't control the words that came out of my mouth.

"FUCK YOU, BRIAN, for putting us through this!"

No one was expecting an opening like that. I hadn't planned to say it – it just came out of my mouth. It is still spoken about today, but with laughter. I could see everyone's relief and thoughts that I'd broken the ice: We would all make it through this. I went on to tell stories and made people laugh, which was what we had wanted. We didn't want a morbid service; we wanted him to be remembered as the happy and funny man that he was. So it was no ordinary service; it was one-of-a-kind, just like him. I finished my eulogy, which left everyone in tears, including myself. Hayley followed, and what a strong, remarkable young lady to speak with such confidence and strength.

The visual was next. We had picked out all the photos, plus we had chosen a couple of special friends to speak on a short video: Peter Pickering, who was one of Brian's oldest mates and Keith Charles, who was also a very special friend to both Brian and me. Keith was unable to make , so we wanted him to speak as we had been great friends for years with a close connection to both of us.

After the service ended, there was a parade of bikes and cars that followed us in the ute. We made one last stop before going to the cemetery. We took him for his last trip through the shed, which he loved more than anything. The Harley in front of us did the biggest burnout possible. He would've loved burning rubber in his shed for the last time for him to see.

We then headed back out onto the road in the procession for everyone to follow. We actually had a police escort which stopped all the traffic all the way through. Because it was such a big funeral, all of the police saluted as we went past, which I thought was very respectful. We all did have a bit of a laugh about Brian having a police escort, considering most of his teenage and adult life had been spent being in trouble from the police – and now he was being escorted by them! We were very grateful to them, though. They were awesome all the way through.

The cemetery was next. The pall bearers were Josh, his nephew, Marcus, and his brothers Steve, Darren, and Bob and Ernie a best mate. I can honestly say I think my heart was ripped out of my body completely as I watched his coffin being lowered into the ground. I felt like I threw it down the grave with him never to return. I never thought in a million years that I would be there that day burying my husband, sitting beside my children as they had to say goodbye to their father.

There were so many people there by the end of it. People meant well, and I was really appreciative, but the line was so big! Everyone had lined up to give us hugs and kisses. We just needed to get to the wake and have a drink.

The Wake

I had organised the Hub to have all the alcohol put in big eskies along each wall to take pressure off the bar. I had also organised Shazz Parsons, who is awesome, to do two servings of food, one early and one later, because when people are pissed and drinking, they need to eat.

I swear, it was the largest and longest wake in history. It didn't end until 1am. The bartender came up to me and said, "Charlie, they won't leave." I soon fixed that. I just went up to them all and said, "Righto, fuckers, it's time to get out. Piss off." And they did. The bartender turned to me and said, "Christ, if I knew you did it that easy, I would have told you an hour ago." I just laughed and went home. I was exhausted, thank God it was all over – for that day at least.

Lastly was the headstone. This is more in-depth than you think. We had to pick the granite and what we wanted written on it. We had his photo put on and then his little plaster man on the side. I wanted it done as soon as possible because I couldn't bear the idea of his grave being there with no one knowing it was him lying in the ground.

When it came to paying all the bills for , I rang Shazz to pay for the catering, but to my shock, it had already been fixed up by a very close friend. You know who you are, and we were very thankful because, believe me, dying isn't cheap!

Josh, Steve, Ernie, Marcus, Darren & Bob around Brian in coffin

Grain Shed 2022

Harley's in funeral procession leaving Grain Shed

People at Grain Shed after service

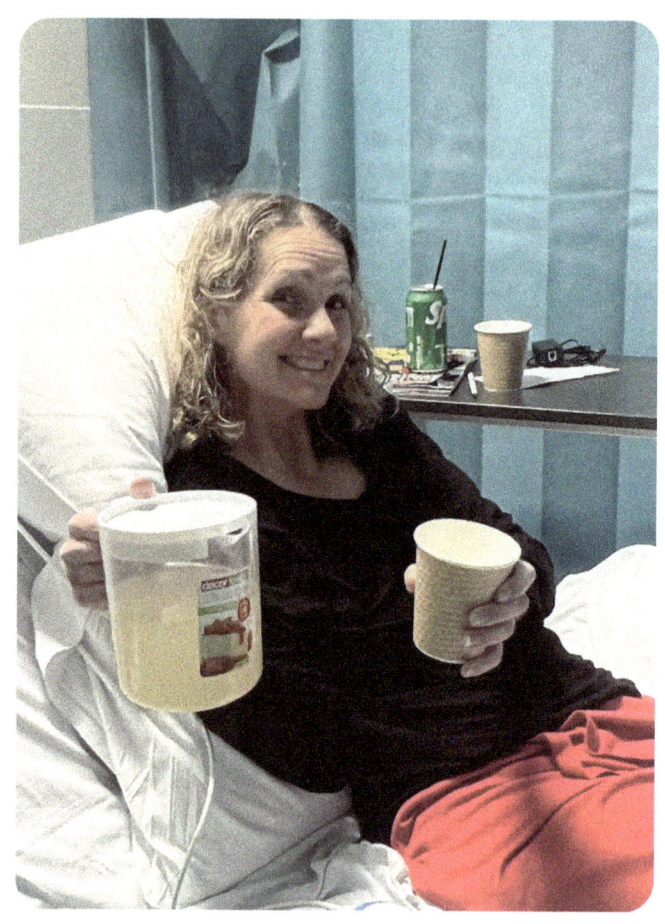

Charlie sick in hospital

Chapter 19:
Getting Sick

"When you have your health, you have everything. When you do not have your health, nothing else matters."

Augensten Burroughs

My journey was far from over. A few weeks after Brian passed, I got sick with chronic diarrhoea that wouldn't stop for weeks. I lost 15kg, which I probably couldn't afford to do, but anyway, by the time I got to see Dr Booth, he took one look at me and organised for me to be flown to Melbourne. Once I got there, I was under the care of all my specialists. They now had to try and find out what was wrong with me.

I had to go have a colonoscopy and drink that awful PicoPrep, which nearly killed me, because I got so dehydrated. But then my heart started beating way too fast. They called the neurologist to the room. Next thing I knew, ICU were standing at the door waiting to take me. This was pretty scary as there were doctors and nurses running everywhere. I didn't know what was happening, but they put some fluids into me and my heart settled... but that wasn't the worst of it.

They had found out that I had a bad bowel infection called C. diff, which can be fatal if not treated properly and quickly. It had made me really sick, and I was put into isolation straight away. The only good thing about it was that it meant I got my own room. Anytime someone came into the room, they had to gown up because it was that

Sonia & Charlie at hospital

infectious. Luckily, we got that under control, and within about a week, I was ready to go home. That was the best news ever.

I was in the Alfred Hospital, the same one as Brian, so I felt his spirit with me the whole time. I was sure he was walking the hallways looking for me… For those who don't believe, you will think this is bullshit; but those of you who do, you will get goosebumps. Before they found the infection, I was lying in bed and felt a poke in my arm, but nobody was there. It happened again. I said, "Okay, Briany. Stop playing games and help me get better." The next morning, they found the infection!

I'm very lucky to have great friends because while I was in hospital in Melbourne for two weeks, I had Marnie, Chelsea, and Sonia come and look after me and visit me constantly.

Chels & Charlie

It was the time of the floods, so I got flown home in the plane by ambulance, which was great, but alas, my journey still hadn't finished. I had been home about a week when I noticed a strange mole had appeared in the middle of my back. I sent a photo through to my GP. Straight away, I got a phone call. I was called in to see him immediately. I knew this couldn't be good news, so I went in. He took a look at it and said, "It looks okay, but I need to cut that out straight away. I think it will be fine."

About a week later, early in the morning, I got a phone call from Dr Booth giving me the news that the mole was actually a melanoma.

Charlie & Marn

Once again, straight back to the doctor – to the surgeon this time – and he had to do a margin cut, which was about 10cm round, to make sure that they got it all. That night, Hayley was graduating, so I didn't tell her I was getting it cut out until I got there. I didn't want to put a dampener on her day while she was getting organised.

I told her and Bob at the table that it had been cut out that day. Hayley looked at me in shock and said, "How many stitches do you have in your back right now, Mum?" I replied, I think there's 10 or 12. But it's okay. I've got enough local anaesthetic in there to numb it until about 10 o'clock, and then I'm going to have to leave because it'll be too painful." Bob looked at me and said, "Who the hell's husband did you fuck up there to have so much bad luck? They just keep raining hell on you." I laughed and said, "I don't know. I wish I did because I wish they would stop. I think I've had more than my fair share." It's someone else's turn now.

Hayley graduated year 12 and she looked absolutely beautiful. I'm so proud of her and I know that her dad would've been smiling down on her, wishing he could've been there.

Charlie, Hayley & Bob at Hy;e's graduation

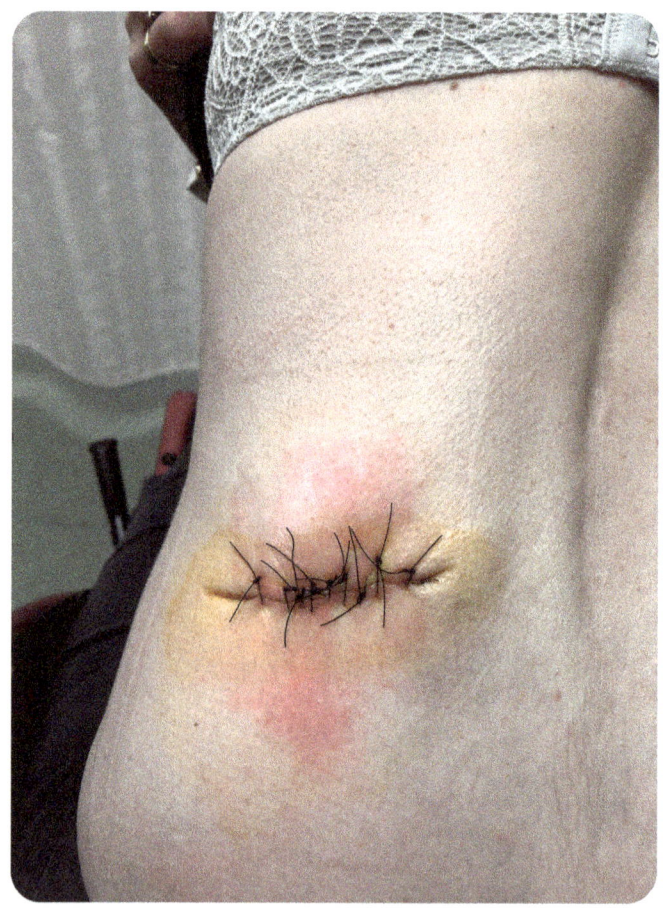

Charlie after my melanoma was removed

Brian's headstone

Annie, Charlie & Monica

Chapter 20:
Grief & Loneliness

"Numbing the pain for a while will make it worse when you finally feel it"
JK. Rowling

Grief is quietly unspoken about, but I am going to give you some insight about the reality of how it affects the body. It's the old saying that grief hits everyone differently, especially when it's such a shock and it's something you are not expecting. Our story wasn't finished, not even close to being the end. I wasn't ready. I wasn't prepared. Now how do I cope? I can't stand not being organised for situations. How do I help my children get through this when I don't even know how I'm going to do it myself? Is grief just a word? What does it mean? All these questions run through my brain constantly.

Sometimes I watch the service on the TV. It makes me feel back there, in the moment again. I don't know why I put myself through that. I think it is to remember how much he was loved. You can still get on and watch it: you just get into O'Hallorans funeral website, pick live stream, type in Brian John Hovenden Jnr, and put in the code 4094.

I had never been faced with anything like this in my entire life. I wouldn't wish it on my worst enemy. It causes torment, chaos, misunderstanding, guilt, anger, sadness, and so many other emotions I can't even explain. You can only run on adrenaline for so long before it is like a big slap in the face of reality landed in your lap – that the world keeps spinning while we are left standing still in our own little world to pick up the pieces that had to be dealt with. I wanted to comfort my children, but we all had the same mindset to keep busy. We actually didn't have a choice but to do this because we had the business to run.

Grief is like a never-ending pit in your heart that never stops. You burst into tears at any time or into a rage of anger that you can't control, and it affects everyone differently. It has been almost three years since Brian passed on the 1st of August, and I think I am only just starting to grieve properly now. I haven't had time to really believe that he is never coming back. I have cried plenty, but haven't accepted till now that he will never walk through my door again, that I will never hear his voice again.

I am angry with the universe, *Why him? WHY?* I just want to scream and yell so loud until I have no voice left, and then just roll into a ball and cry. But then, I regain my composure, pull myself together, and let my stronger self reappear to take over and let my determination kick back in. I can't fall apart for too long. I am relied on by my children, amongst others. I don't often let people see the real me. I believe it leaves me weak and too vulnerable.

Loneliness

Loneliness is a silent killer that eats away at your insides until you are nothing left but a shell of your body: bones covered in skin and clothes. There is nothing left but memories and dreams of the touch of a kiss and a warm body lying beside you. Instead, you are left with an empty bed, sitting at a table, eating tea by yourself every night – then it becomes easier to just not eat.

I hate the 1st of every month because it is just a reminder that yet another month has passed without him. I start getting antsy around the 29th because I know it is coming up. Then of course, you have all the anniversaries, birthdays, wedding anniversary, and Christmas. All the celebrations are never the same again. People that tell you it gets easier as time goes by. Bullshit. That doesn't happen. Sorry, but the truth is out. The only comfort I have is that he is watching over us all the time, and he would have serious FOMO (fear of missing out) on anything.

The day Brian died so did a huge part of me. I am broken and feel that I can never be repaired. When part of your soul leaves your body, it just disappears into open space, floating around out of reach for you to try and grab. It is a feeling that words can't describe.

I feel guilty if I am happy, even though I know he wouldn't want me to. So when I finally do feel any kind of happiness, I push people away it's just what I always have done. I think it is a protective barrier I put up. It has cost me dearly because I think I have lost chances of having anyone in my life that might actually care about me. Unfortunately, that is just my first reaction.

Imagine coming home to an empty house every night, full of photos and memories of sitting out on the verandah having a few drinks before tea. The thought of never being able to do this again makes me cry every time I think about it.

Losing your best friend and soul mate all at once can be very overwhelming. I couldn't even change his pillowcase for a year. I never washed it, just folded it and put it away. Some nights I still sleep in his shirt to try and still smell him for some comfort. I think the worst possible thing of being alone is going to sleep every night with that side of the bed empty: you reach your arm over in the middle of the night and it is cold. No one's there.

I haven't been able to pack away any of his clothes. They are all still in his cupboard. I can't tell you when the right time to do this is because I just simply don't know.

It is lonely having no one to talk to, someone that completely understands you with no judgement. I have gone from having someone who needed me 24/7 for over 20 years to no one.

I cried in the shower every day. I still do because I miss him so much.

I live with the guilt every day that it should have been me instead of him. He was the fit one, and I am the useless one that has a fucked body and not good for anything or anyone. It should have been me. I can't say that or stop believing that enough. It is something that stays in my head every day, just feeling worthless. I won't come across this way if you ever meet me because I bury it deeply. It's just for me to know and touch.

I have been through hell and back, physically and mentally. The things that the mind thinks about would make your boggle, and guilt is something that never leaves you.

After losing Brian, I lost my great friend, my GP, Dr Booth. When I went and said goodbye, he asked to see me. So still dealing with the loss of my husband, then I had to say goodbye to another close friend. I am also very close with his wife, Gaye.

Honestly, I can't tell you which is worse: being able to hold hands and say goodbye, knowing they are about to die, or not being able to say goodbye because they are taken without warning? So once again, I shed tears, but I had to wipe them away and be strong and courageous.

I listen to a lot of music now. It is the way I communicate. It lets people know exactly how I feel. The song *Broken* by Jonah Kagen sums me up perfectly.

I also pretend a lot that I am fine. I put on a brave face, smile, and stay strong. I rarely show my true self. Only very few people see the broken-down Charlie. I had a good friend ask me why I needed to pretend to my best friends. Well, the answer is that it is easier to let people think you are fine – although, it takes more energy to do this. But I need to always show strength and save the tears and anger for myself...

I used to punch my leg repeatedly until it bruised. It was just a way to release anger, and it worked for a short time, until my daughter saw me doing it. Then I stopped.

Once again, just another hurdle I jumped and made it over. My strength took over. My body has endured more pain physically and emotionally than most people will go through in their whole life. That's why I am living proof that you can overcome all these obstacles and fears.

I just have to say one thing that freaks me out is when I go to the cemetery and look at the headstone. I see the blank part on the other side where my name is to go. This is very confronting, just staring at that space, knowing that it is mine, just sitting there... waiting for me to die. Well, sorry, husband, I love you more than life itself, but you are not getting me for quite a while yet. I still have shit to do and I will tell you all about it once I'm done.

Carol, Isla, Charlie, Lisa A, Glenda & Lisa K

Chapter 21:
Friends' Connection Post-Passing

"Anyone can show up when you're happy. But the ones who stay by your side when your heart falls apart. They are your true friends"

Brigitte Nicole

Another huge fear I had after Brian passed was thinking I would lose everyone. I didn't think his friends would stick around and support myself and the children. I couldn't have been more wrong. It was actually the complete opposite. They were all there whenever we needed them, all of the time, just a phone call away. I can never thank them enough. I knew they were always Brian's friends, but they were mine too. I just didn't realise how much we meant to them and how much they meant to us.

We stayed close with Brian's youngest brother, Bob, his wife, Kylie, my nieces, Milla and Miah, and then my other nephew, Michael, his partner, Cassie, and their five kids. Brian's favourite trick to teach all his nieces and nephews was to put the rude finger up, which he did from when they were a very young age. I know he will be laughing about this.

Lisa Keating, who would have to be my best friend here, has a little radar on me. I swear, every time I am having a bad day, she turns up. She is so special to me, words can't express enough. Monica, Aunty Kylie, Aunty Cinta, Uncle Danny, Carinda, and Fluffa aren't far behind. I call on all of them to help me through the saddest times of my life.

Then there are all the uncles, as we call them, Bob, Ernie, JD, Dill, Franko, Browny, Matto. These are just to name a few, but we would never have made it through this without them all. I also have to make a special mention to Aunty Paula, Uncle Chris and all their eleven kids, especially Shani, Emma, Jesse, Jade, Rhys, Jake, and Darcy.

There are so many special friends. I can't name them all here, but I know I could ring any of them, day or night, and they would be here. I will always have my best friends from school, who are life-long friends, and luckily for me, as you get older, friendship groups change, and the circle becomes larger. Honestly, you can never have enough friends.

Charlie & Ellis nieces and nephews

Friends' Connection Post-Passing

Brian, Lisa & Ernie

Charlie & Lisa Keating

Danny, Chris, Paula, Jacinta & Charlie

Shane, Dill, Lisa & Franko

Dill & JD

Fierce and Unstoppable

Monica & Charlie

Briany's day 2024 at Mystic Park Pub

Personalised ring

Chapter 22:
Remembering Him

'Those we love never truly leave us. There are things that death cannot touch"

Jack Thorne

Brian will never be forgotten. He will always be a part of us. My heart will always belong to him. He was very well known for his favourite beer, Carlton Light, or cat's piss, as Danny called it! I liked that he drank light beer because I always used to drink heavy beer, then wine, so I never had to drive. His other favourite drink was Stones & Dry.

He will always be remembered for his glasses. He wore them hung around his neck, and they clicked together when he sat them on his nose. He thought it was a great party trick for the kids and some adults.

Everyone who ever met him loved him. He just had that cheeky personality that stayed with people. Plus, he loved to know all the gossip Monday mornings with the workers was his highlight for the week.

I miss his call at 8 o'clock every morning to say hello. He would FaceTime me to try and catch me as I got out of the shower, bloody old perv. Now Hayley calls me at 9 o'clock instead, but not FaceTime… She always kept his head shaved and, to her credit, his ears and nose. The radio has to be left on for the puppies, that was his rule. So, we still do that for him.

Fierce and Unstoppable

Brian's memorial plaque at home

Anyone who knew Brian well knew he loved to fart and used to do it on the kids' heads. They all snuck around doing this. It became a game. This one day, Brian pulled over a chair while Josh was sitting on the couch. He stood up on the chair, pulled his pants down, leant over the couch slipped, fell, and nearly landed on Josh's head. We were all laughing so hard, and still do today, as I am while I am writing this. We weren't the most conventional family, but we had fun. Brian and I were pretty relaxed parents until the kids mucked up, and then I had to be the disciplinary one.

We have started a Memorial Day for him every year in early August called Brian's Day. We get the boys on their bikes; we get his Chevvys

Briany's day 2025 Lake Boga pub

out, go to a pub for lunch, then gather back at home for drinks to remember him.

I had his wedding ring resized so I could wear it, but now I just wear it around my neck so he is never away from me.

I still have the blue plastic hospital bag with his belongings he had with him on his last day. This is shoved at the back of his cupboard, which I do pull out regularly just to cry and remember him and to hold him close. My heart broke that day and will never repair. I'm sure Josh and Hayley's did too.

Anyone who knows and meets me will soon recognise that I love jewellery. I wear approximately 30 rings on my fingers and many bracelets. Most of them have significant memories as Brian bought them all. He used to take me to Melbourne every Christmas to the Boxing Day sales, so I could buy whatever I wanted. He would just wait out the front of the shop while I went in. He loved seeing me with all my jewellery on.

Charlie in the Chev at Briany's day 2025

One year on our way home, there was this one ring I couldn't decide on, so I didn't get it. As we were driving past the shop on our way out of the city, he pulled the car over and made me go back to the shop and buy it. Another day I had been in Barham after I had been into pathology. I was at my favourite little shop over there, Jewellery on the Move. I tried a ring on that I loved but didn't buy it. I told Brian about it when I got home. The next morning was a Saturday, and he told me to get up and get ready. He was taking me for a drive. He took me to Barham to buy the ring. He could be quite the romantic and, of course, he was rewarded for it.

I will always remember his love, kindnesses, and humour. I had a ring specially made with the letter *B* and *C* with both our birthstones in it as a symbol of our bond. This same jeweller made my 40th bracelet, which Brian put 40 diamonds in. I wear both of these pieces every day.

His old employees reminded me of all the jokes he used to play and how much fun they used to have. There are so many stories of this man I could fill a whole other book, but those memories are held by everybody who knew him. He left an impression on everyone.

Michael, Cassie & family with Charlie

We used to hold all the kids' parties at our house. It was the perfect party house. Josh used to have his mates over every weekend around the fire, while Hayley held bigger parties with all her friends. Briany loved when they left all their drinks behind because he would drink them. When they came back next time, they were all gone! The next morning, he loved cooking them all a big feed of bacon and eggs, even if they were too hungover to eat it. All the kids called me Mumma Hovo, and they still do when I see them, which I love.

I can't ignore the life Brian had before we met, and I know I don't know the half of it. He loved his mates and had a pretty good party life I'm told. I don't know a lot of the stories, so the ones who do will have to remember them themselves.

Although Brian always spoke about his times with Noel. One time, they were drunk and thought it would be a great idea to take the

Harley out, but they had no helmets, so they got two black plastic pot plants, cut eyes out, and wore them instead.

Another time, Noel was in a fight, so Brian picked the bloke up and put him in the bin, headfirst. Briany loved telling the kids his stories. Another was when their group was in an ongoing feud with another group. They had all had a punch on, but then they went home, got a shotgun, came back, and blew the windscreen out of their car. This feud went on for years.

He used to get into a fair bit of fun and trouble with Terry: fighting, bikes, drinking, and fast cars.

I think one of his favourites was telling them when he told his partner at the time he was going to get fish and chips for tea, but instead, he jumped in a truck with his mate, Spana, and went to Adelaide. Needless to say, he was not very popular when he got home.

Peter Pickering was another who was one of his best mates, and they had a lot of fun too.

Like I said, there are many stories, and he did enjoy his life. If I let Ant, Ernie, and the Castlemaine boys go, they would go for days.

I did organise a surprise 40th party for Brian and, bloody hell, what a mission that was, trying to keep secrets away from him as he was so nosey about everything all the time. On the day of the party, it was Bob's job to try and keep him busy while we got everything organised. Bob told me if I ever did that to him, then he would kill me. We were at home getting everything ready, and I got a text from Bob – Brian bloody reckons he needs to check something at home!

So Kylie and I were throwing food into cupboards to try and hide it. Then, when he got there, we had to try and act normal. This happened a couple of times. I had gone in to pick up the cake, and he turned up. This was while the boys were putting up the tent too. Steve turned around and told Brian to fuck off and get out of here… so he obviously knew that something was happening beforehand anyway. And then, at the end of the day, when he was supposed to come home? He wouldn't!

I had to ring him and tell him to get his arse home. That's just what he was like, practical joker all the time. But when he did turn up, he still did get a surprise by the number of people that were there. His cake was the best, though, because it was actually a pair of tits.

So I do have lots of happy memories about our relationship and the family in the house farm. It was all great. Nobody can ever take your memories away from you, so hold onto them as long as you possibly can.

Briany's day 2023

Charlie & Noel

Brian & chev

Brian

Brian

Chapter 23:
My Dark Thoughts

"When you face difficult times, know that challenges are not sent to destroy you. They're sent to promote, increase, and strengthen you."

Joel Osteen

Now for a real insight to who I really am and my deepest darkest thoughts. I am a person with a very deep personality who loves, cares, and hates to the core. I love a good time and love to party. Plus, I swear like a trooper – if you haven't already guessed – and I don't care who it's in front of. That is just me. If you don't like it, too bad. If I love you, it comes with purity, loyalty, passion, and strength to protect you to the end of time. I care very deeply and will do so with all my heart. Friendship is everything to me and one of the most important things in life. Without that, what is the point of being here?

But on the other hand, if you are my enemy, I will make it my mission to make you very unhappy. It is either black or white with me – no grey in between. As my cousin says, when someone upsets or pisses me off, you can see my brain plotting the revenge before the incident has even occurred or finished! I have a temper that goes from zero to 100 in seconds, and you will never be left wondering what I'm thinking.

My pet hate is when people don't reply on Snapchat or Messenger when asked a question, and I can see it's been opened. It drives me insane and it's just rude.

Now that you know a little bit about me, we can get into the nitty-gritty of how my brain works. It never switches off. It thinks 24/7 with every scenario you can think of running through it. I often get accused of overthinking things. I don't see it this way, rather it's my way of seeing through things and seeing the whole truth, because it just runs through over and over until the answer is revealed.

I have been through hell and back, I'm sure. I don't quite know how I have deserved this, all in all. I thought I was a decent person. But maybe not, maybe I did have it coming to me. But if I did, do it to me, not my children.

I have been lucky enough to have been given MS. I can't walk. I'm in a wheelchair. I had a melanoma. I was made a widow at 44. If that is not enough to make you think the darkest of thoughts about putting plans in place of how to end your life, I don't know what is. Just wishing one day you don't wake up and how it would be a blessing for everyone. I often feel worthless and who in their right mind would ever find me attractive or would want someone in a wheelchair or that needs someone who can't look after themselves?

Being called a widow feels weird and not real. I've since found out there is a box on medical forms to tick "widow". This was very confronting the first time I was called to do it. Then there are all the little things that tip you off over and over again. For instance, cancelling his phone. I had to produce the death certificate along with ambulance cover. Then there was health insurance and Medicare.

I am now classed as a single. It would be different if it was by choice, but when you are forced to do this shit, it becomes overwhelming. I broke down to the operator and couldn't even speak. But once again, pull the big girl pants up, and just do what has to be done. These are the times I reach out for help and strength from family and friends to weather the storm.

Three years later, I am still receiving mail and phone calls for him. The thing that fucked me off the most was once he had passed, the ATO sent me a tax bill for him. Fuck, I was angry about that. Charlie Devil was on her tiptoes that day.

Feeling useless is a terrible way to feel about yourself, but when you are having a bad day, these are all the things that cross your mind constantly. I am usually a very confident person, but we can all slip and hide our deepest fears.

Sometimes the pain, mentally and physically, seems too hard to bear. One day, I am walking; the next, I'm in a wheelchair. I just wish it would end, and those dark thoughts sneak back in. But I am here to tell you: lean on your best friends or the people you trust most. Cry a river. It is healthy to release that pain. It feels good.

Just remember, no matter how bad it seems, there is always your inner strength shining through to pull you from the darkness and back into the light. We all have too much to live for and too much life left to enjoy. Stay strong and find a new path to follow. It may take you to greatness. That is what I am doing now: eyes on the prize.

Charlie & Army man in Hawaii

Girls at home 2022

Chapter 24:
Moving Forward vs Moving On

"If you don't like the road you're walking, start paving another one."
Dolly Parton

Brian can never be replaced as my best friend or soul mate, but I have concluded that he would want me to be happy. I call it moving forward, not moving on. I have no regrets in our relationship as there was nothing left unsaid. So, it was two-and-a half years later when I decided it was time to maybe find a male friend with benefits. Brian's favourite saying was, "It was too high off the ground to eat grass!" I thought I would dip my toe in the water, but instead of swimming, I think I fucking drowned... This was a huge decision for me. I hadn't been with another man for 25 years.

I found an old friend. It was fun and the company was nice. It was good to have someone to talk to. But there was a fair bit of confusion about what the situation was, neither of us wanted a relationship we both made that very clear from the start. We were supposed to stay friends, but that doesn't always happen. It was just a flingy thingy and a distraction from my real life. But for a moment, I saw what it was like to smile and be happy again. It was something where we had contact several times a day for months either by Snapchat or phone. He made me feel needed and wanted, but then at the flip of a coin worthless at the same time.

I was not used to this, and I normally would never let anyone make me feel that way. I am very strong-minded and opinionated, so I surprised

Charlie in Hawaii

myself that I allowed that to happen. I've just put it down as a learning curve. I think I was just vulnerable, lonely, and stupid. I got swept up into a whirlwind of make-believe. It was a mutual agreement, but the lines got blurred somewhere along the way I think we had different definitions of friends with benefits, and you find out the hard way: people aren't who you think they really are. I was not completely innocent in this situation as I always ask too many questions and have too much to say. I was also naïve as it was the first time I had been with anyone since Brian and very unsure how to navigate these waters and I'm sure I made some wrong turns along the way.

Moving Forward vs Moving On

Girls at Swan Hill races in 2023

I will just recognise this as part of my journey to my new life and a fling that was fun, but not great either. I am not going to waste any more words on this; I just want women in my situation to be mindful of what you are getting yourself into. If you just want a fuck buddy just fuck them and fuck them off don't let it become anything else ha ha ….

My next adventure was to go to Hawaii with my two closest cousins, Maree and Sarah, who are more like sisters. We flew business class, and I'm sorry, no poverty-flying ever again. What an experience! Plus, for once, being disabled has its advantages. You get special treatment, which is awesome.

I started doing daily vlogs, which the girls hated. I loved it, and so did all our followers on Facebook, so now everywhere I go this will happen. Our trip was great. We had a big learning curve about the culture of tipping in America. The wine was shit so we drank pina coladas, and I

Girls at races 2025

became quite partial to gin. We also experienced Hawaiian traditions. It was a great experience and has now given us the travel bug. There is so much to see and do. Life is too short to do it all!

My next trip was to Perth, just with Maree this time. We were basically there to catch up with friends. It was fantastic. JD and Jeannette lived in Mandurah, which is about an hour out of Perth. It's a beautiful little place. Our accommodation was awesome. We walked out the door and we were practically at a pub, which was perfect. We stayed here for four days. They drove us and showed us around and treated us like royalty. It was nice just to spend time with old friends. We did have one rest day of sitting out on the balcony, enjoying the view and quite a few beverages.

Maree, Charlie & Sarah in Hawaii

Next, we were off to Perth to see Keithy and Claire, who used to live in Swan Hill but moved to Perth to be closer to their daughter and grandchildren. I was so excited to see these guys as they hold a special place in my heart. We have been close for years and years. I look at them as people I can confide in and trust. If I'm ever feeling shit and need to laugh, I ring Keithy. He always cheers me up.

While we were there we got to catch up with Zoe, Judd, and their kids – plus, Thud dropped in. A few hours turned into a whole day of drinking and laughing. We were, once again, made to feel very welcome. We got to catch up with them one more time for lunch before we left. This trip I would rate so far as one of the best.

Part of my new look on life means I am going to make the most of it while I can and just live life to the fullest. I spoke to all my old girlfriends, and we decided we needed to catch up more often. Our first group catch-up was here at home, which was another fun day. Then we

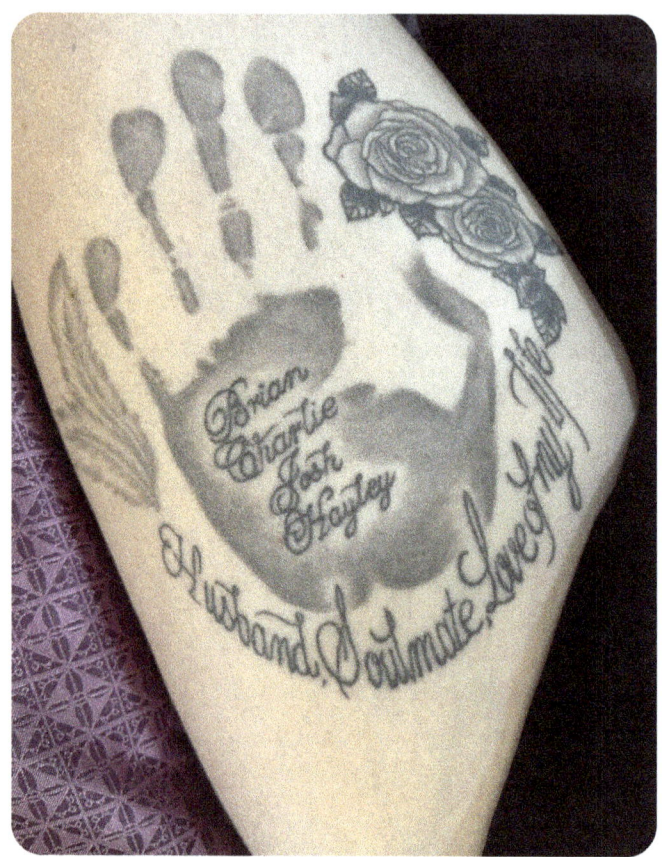

Thigh tattoo of Brian's handprint

decided the June races were to be our next get-together. We have been doing that for three years now. The first two years I had a marquee, but this year, a lot of people couldn't make it, so we downsized into a marquee that was already there.

As it turned out, I ended up in hospital two weeks prior with Covid, but I was still determined to make it. I only got out of hospital two days prior and, believe it or not, I wasn't drinking. Nobody could believe it. They knew I must have been crook, but I just wanted to spend time with my dear friends, Chels, Sonia, Carms, Kymm, and Shelley. I also got to catch up with my bestie, KP. So it was well worth the effort.

Moving Forward vs Moving On

Never Give Up tattoo

I have another dear friend that calls in and checks on me regularly, Bully – he is a best friend and tries to keep me on track, doesn't he have his work cut out for him !! I've known him over 30 years, we go back a long way… Wig and Isla are others, plus Brian's trusty old mate, Noel. These guys were all great mates of Brian. Jika calls in weekly to check on me. He's like a father to me. I also have another one of those, but he lives in Perth - Keithy , so I FaceTime them and talk to them regularly.

My next path I took was to coach netball again – the B grade out at Lalbert. I had gone home again to all my family and friends. The

Claire, Keithy, Charlie, Maree, Zoe & Judd

coaching gig was a lifeline thrown to me to get my life back on track, stop wallowing in my own shit, and realise there is a big world out there to enjoy. I loved coaching the girls; it made me feel alive again. We didn't win many games, but we did the best we could. I put my hand up to coach the next year, but I was given the arse. I suppose we didn't win much and they thought I didn't cut the mustard – plus, not being able to run around and show them what I meant.

I was absolutely devastated. One-year-wonder – how embarrassing. I don't think they realised how important it was to my life. Anyway, moving forward: one door closes; another one opens. If that hadn't happened, I wouldn't be writing this book, which means more to me

Moving Forward vs Moving On

Hayley & Josh's 18th & 21st birthday dinner 2022

than coaching. I am still involved because Hayley is still playing. I am thankful because it did bring new people into my life, like Megan, who is like another daughter to me. Her family are special to me too and help me at the drop of a hat. Megan calls me Mum, and her kids call me Grams.

I believe people are brought into our lives for different reasons, sometimes a short time, sometimes for a long time. She was brought to me because I needed someone extra in our family and she is the one.

Then there is Ethel, Hayley's best friend, again, another one who calls me Mum. If you need someone to make you laugh, she is your girl. I

Mark (tattooist) & Charlie

just love her! If you haven't worked out by now, I have an enormous group of friends and family, and I am an aunty to so many, which I absolutely love.

Another dream I have is to get into is public speaking, which I love doing. I have spoken a few times about my life with MS, but there is so much more to my life to tell. I need to get awareness out there about so many topics that people need to know. Just give me a microphone, and I will take it from there. I am a person with a disability, I have run businesses, I am a mother, and now, I am an author. I feel I have

Charlie & Keithy

a lot to say about life and experiences. I have led a colourful life and I am happy to share.

I also took up another hobby of getting tattoos, which I find to be a kind of therapy. I have Brian on me, his hand, and plenty more that tells a story. My tattooist is Mark Bretherton in Bendigo. He has become a good friend and someone I feel I could ask for help at any time without question.

As I draw to the end, unfortunately, I have sad news that we have decided to sell the business. It breaks my heart, and it was a very emotional decision to make. It was the dream Briany and I had built, with the kids in tow all the way. But alas, everything has to come to an end.

I'm so sorry, Briany, but it's just too hard without you. I'm sick of making every decision on my own, not knowing whether I'm doing the right thing or not. It is time for Josh to follow his trade and actually

Marn, Penny & Charlie

go out on his own. He was landed into Brian's shoes without choice; Hayley was always on call to help when needed. I have been there for 25 years, and it is now time for me to look after my health and enjoy life. As I said, it's very emotional. It is the end of an era, but it will never be forgotten. Who knows? That might be my next book – about all my travels, living life, and happiness.

My last message is stay strong: find the resilience and determination within you that you didn't even know you had. Have confidence and believe in yourself. Keep your friends close and your enemies closer, it is how you will survive.

I talk about inspiration a lot. Well, it brings tears to my eyes knowing I have at least inspired my 13-year-old niece, Miah, who I love to the stars and back. She wrote an essay in English about someone who inspired you, and she wrote about her Aunty Charlie – that I taught

Moving Forward vs Moving On

Girls at races 2024

her never to give up. It made me feel so special and touched my heart. This just reminds me how important it is to keep fighting, to make an impact on other people's lives in a positive way.

Over and out and catch you on the flip side xxoo

Signing off till next time,
Charlie xx

A song to inspire you is ***"She stands up"*** by *Women Empowerment*.

Listen and be strong x

KP & Charlie

Charlie & Ethel

Moving Forward vs Moving On

Charlie & Megan

Lisa, Charlie & Isla

Charlie & Bully

Charlie & JD

Charlie & Hayley

Conclusion

I can't believe I've actually finished writing my first book. It is something that was very emotionally challenging but gratifying at the same time. It is my bare-all true story to the world, to put out there for everyone to see. To show everyone that someone like me, an ordinary human being, can go through all these challenges that have been given to me… And still survive.

The message that I want you to leave with is that anything is possible if you put your mind to it. You can have your whole body ripped apart, but it's up to you to put it back together. Your mind, body, and soul connection is a very powerful thing. Power of the mind is what people don't count on – they don't realise how strong it can be. Prove to yourself that you have the endurance and courage to push through every challenge that is put in your way.

Life was never meant to be easy, but as I said, there is always light at the end of the tunnel. And if you believe, there is always someone's hand there, to pull you through the darkness back into the light. They will bring you out the other side a stronger and more determined person than ever. Don't ever stop believing in yourself, no matter what anyone tells you.

I have a fire that burns inside of me, and it burns right to my core.

But fire is a good thing.

It's the flame that keeps going and never burns out.

It keeps you alive.

Laughter is the best medicine in the world, laugh so hard until your cheeks and your belly hurt. There is nothing that warms the heart more and to put a smile back on your face than this sort of happiness. Remember, it costs nothing to say hello and smile, and, hopefully, that will put a smile on someone else's face.

Acknowledgements

As sad as it is for me to say this, I would firstly like to thank my loving husband, Brian John Hovenden, for giving me the opportunity, strength, and courage to write this book. If it wasn't for, you this would never have happened. I wish circumstances were different and you were able to read this book and that I was writing it about a different story. Instead, it is about you, my love.

The man, the myth, the legend. You are truly loved by everyone who came in contact with you, and that is why I want the world to know everything about you, never to be forgotten.

Secondly, thank you to my children, Josh and Hayley, because once again, without you, without your support, this would not have been at all possible. I do apologise for some things. You may not want to read about your mother, but anyway, as I said: it is just life.

I think one of the people that I am most grateful to is Emily Gowor, my mentor, who gave me the support, encouragement, and confidence to make me believe in myself, that I was capable of actually writing this book, and that my story needed to be told and heard.

J, from the minute we first made contact, I knew that we were kindred spirits, both with spiritual beliefs about what is possible to achieve in our lives. You make me feel that I can make all my dreams come true.

To my friends, Isla Delmenico, Lisa Keating, and Kerry Barry, who encouraged me and gave me the idea that I was capable of writing my story and made me believe that people needed to hear it. So, to these lovely ladies, you have my full gratitude of making this all possible.

Finally, thank you to you, the readers, for taking time to show an interest and want to hear my story.

www.ingramcontent.com/pod-product-compliance
Lightning Source LLC
Chambersburg PA
CBHW042317090526
44583CB00024BA/3018